ONCE UPON
A RHYME

IMAGINATION FOR
A NEW GENERATION

North London
Edited by Heather Killingray

 Young**Writers**

First published in Great Britain in 2004 by:
Young Writers
Remus House
Coltsfoot Drive
Peterborough
PE2 9JX
Telephone: 01733 890066
Website: www.youngwriters.co.uk

SB ISBN 1 84460 456 X

Foreword

Young Writers was established in 1991 and has been passionately devoted to the promotion of reading and writing in children and young adults ever since. The quest continues today. Young Writers remains as committed to engendering the fostering of burgeoning poetic and literary talent as ever.

This year's Young Writers competition has proven as vibrant and dynamic as ever and we are delighted to present a showcase of the best poetry from across the UK. Each poem has been carefully selected from a wealth of *Once Upon A Rhyme* entries before ultimately being published in this, our twelfth primary school poetry series.

Once again, we have been supremely impressed by the overall high quality of the entries we have received. The imagination, energy and creativity which has gone into each young writer's entry made choosing the best poems a challenging and often difficult but ultimately hugely rewarding task - the general high standard of the work submitted amply vindicating this opportunity to bring their poetry to a larger appreciative audience.

We sincerely hope you are pleased with our final selection and that you will enjoy *Once Upon A Rhyme North London* for many years to come.

Contents

Grazebrook Primary School, Stoke Newington

Jubilee Primary School, Stoke Newington

Charlotte Joseph (8)	57
Aamenah Mulla (10)	57
Bryher Litten Beatty (8)	58
Maariyah Dawood (9)	58
Dayna Wyatt (8)	59
Junaid Vahed (11)	59
Joshua Joseph (9)	60
Kaddel Durowoju (9)	61
Candice Elias (10)	61
Justin Cunningham (9)	62
Joel Titley (8)	63
Klaudia Barys (9)	64
Amirah Facey (9)	65
Patrick Narine-Turnbull (7)	65
James Moore (8)	66
Humza Sheikh (7)	66
Itunu Alimi (8)	67
Zoe Rasbash (7)	67
Leigh Charles (11)	68
Sabina Rahman (11)	68
Martha Cusker (8)	69
Tejas Patel (10)	69
Nell Ranken-Perrott (8)	70
Francesca Titley (10)	71
Tiffany William (9)	71
Leah Abraham (9)	72
Naeema Teladia (10)	72
Nazia Ahmed (10)	73
Kiranjit Kaur Chohan (9)	73
Andres Nino (9)	74
Precious Couprie-Matra (10)	74
Kainoni Brown-Jones (9)	75
Liam Pegram (10)	75
Wesley Frankel (10)	75
Ruth Leah Shorten (9)	76
Shenae Bristol (10)	76
Joseph Idris (10)	77
Sam Green Dorado (10)	77
Bianca Mesuria (11)	78
Gabriella George (11)	78
Zarah Mann (10)	79

Ismail Marshall (11)   79
Zayed Boyd (11)   80

Kerem School, Hampstead Garden Suburb
Samuel Collins (10)   81
Jack Wagner (10)   81
Yasmin Judah (9)   82
Andrea Edelman (9)   82
Oliver Collins (9)   83
Raymond Hanassab (10)   83
Rachel Kahn (10)   84
Kathryn Moses (11)   84
Gabriella Suissa (10)   85
Ilana Green (10)   85
Gideon Harris (9)   86
Emily Gittelmon (11)   86
Liora Fox (10)   87
David Gottlieb (9)   88
Joseph Greenwall-Cohen (10)   89
Sabrina Zeloof (9)   90
Solomon Ishack (11)   91
Yael Yamin-Joseph (10)   92
Lillie Miller (11)   92
Laura Baker (11)   93
Ariella Aghai (10)   94
Naomi Revel (9)   95
Arthur Caplin (10)   96

Nightingale Primary School, Wood Green
Leanne Webb-Mills (11)   96
Jackie Moore (11)   97
Sean Gallagher (8)   97
Geniene Miller (10)   98
Shanice Clarke (7)   98
Shamika Davis (9)   99
Taylor Stoakes (9)   99
Allisia Ngbanzo (11)   100
Stavros Zangoulos (7)   100
Jack Twomey (9)   101
Shani Thompson-Ellis (10)   101
Omar Ibrahim (10)   102

The Poems

Chewed And Spewed

I suddenly saw a glimpse of light as the paper fell away.
A big, dark figure loomed over me, as I saw the light of day.
He stuck me in a huge, dark hole and bounced me up and down.
He smashed and crashed and bashed and thrashed and mashed
me all around.

All at once, I was shot right out and landed on the floor.
I guess the giant creature didn't want me anymore.
Another creature squished me flat and carried me about,
But when the creature saw me there, it went into a pout.

With a stick he scraped me off, so I supposed that I was done.
He threw me in a rubbish bin with the other bubblegum.

Jack Begert (10)

Nature

Nature is all God's creations
Nature is animals
Nature is people
Nature is weather
Nature is living things.

Matt Ilunga (11)

Like Me

I am like the White Witch of Narnia,
Sitting on her golden throne,
Ruling over everything,
Ruling over everyone.

My kindness is like a fluttering feather,
Flying over the starlit sky,
Then hidden by a dark, grey cloud,
My anger comes again.

My sorrow is as sad as seeing an old man's corpse,
Lying in a coffin dead still,
Then he slowly rises and walks away,
And my grief is gone forever.

My joy is as happy as a newborn baby,
With her one little tiny strand of hair,
Then she suddenly speaks, 'Mama, Dada,'
And I'm happier than ever before.

Martha Sanderson (10)
Canonbury Primary School, Islington

The Killer

She's got sinister cat eyes
And evil thoughts,
Like the mythical creature
Medusa.
Ever since she was a little girl,
She'd never cried.
Shall I tell you why?
She saw a lot of tragedy.
She became vicious like a pitbull,
She would chop your head off,
Then wipe the blood off.
You've got a minute to pray
And a second to die.

Papillon Bond Williams (9)
Canonbury Primary School, Islington

Looking For A Friend

I'm looking for a friend, a best friend
Someone just like me
Someone good at football
Someone smart and free
Someone special
Quite good looking too
Someone rich and true
Someone extremely clever
Someone who likes the things I like
Someone nice and kind
Someone really new
Quite good at rugby too
That kind of special person
Perhaps you?

Matt Oakley (9)
Canonbury Primary School, Islington

I Will Put In My Box . . .

I will put in my box . . .
The first tear of a terrified baby
The blood of the Devil himself
And the feather from a phoenix.

I will put in my box . . .
The howl of a free wolf
The sound of the sea lapping against the rocks
And the heart of an eagle that once swept through the sky.

My box is made out of the eyes of a puppy
The wings from a butterfly
And the antennae from a stick insect.

Sorcha Gillbert-Dillon (10)
Canonbury Primary School, Islington

I Am Better

My mum's prettier than your mum
She shops at Tiffany's too
My mum's richer than your mum
I am much better than you.

My dad's better than your dad
My dad has more money too
My dad drives a cooler car
He drives a sports car too
I am much better than you.

My brother's better than your brother
His listens to better music than you
My brother's better than your brother
He's got two girlfriends too
My brother's better than your brother
I am much better than you.

Now here the poem stops
And while she gabbled
A lion from the zoo
Came up and ate her whole
Sad - ahh! No!

Catherine Lynch (10)
Canonbury Primary School, Islington

My Dog

My smart dog is as brainy as a cheetah for his food.
His long tail is as fluffy as a white cloud.
He has black ears as pointed as a rocky mountain.
His long bark is as noisy as a volcano erupting.

Edward Hartill
Frith Manor Primary School, Lullington Garth

The Fire

The fire slithered
Along the narrow school corridor
Licking the paper
Melting the glass
Biting the lights
Like a hungry crocodile.
Puffs of smoke
Coloured the legs of the large building.
Firemen came
And taught the fire a lesson.
'Do not mess with us,
You'll regret it'
The hoses seemed to gush.
The fire shouted,
'You'll never catch us,
We're too fast.'
But it was wrong.
It got caught
And sizzled to death!

Nishil Shah (11)
Frith Manor Primary School, Lullington Garth

I Saw A Cat

I saw a fluffy cat wearing a brown coat as fluffy as candyfloss
Her long, silky tail is as long as a rat's
Her sparkling, black eyes are as bright as a diamond
Her long legs moving as smooth as a tiger.

Tomomi Shinomiya (10)
Frith Manor Primary School, Lullington Garth

Mountain Heaven!

I saw a grey mountain,
A shining pinnacle in the sky,
Where the great eagles fly,
Standing high above the ground,
A great treasure inside is to be found.

Excitement brewing up inside me,
My first step, it seems an eternity,
My shaky hand reaching for an icy stone,
Now me and the mountain shall fight alone.

Watching cascading icy water,
My mind begins to falter!
Oxygen is scarce here,
Now the only feeling I possess is fear.

My heart a beating drum,
The sky is now glum,
But victory befalls me,
I have climbed the tallest mountain you see!

Amir Hussain (10)
Frith Manor Primary School, Lullington Garth

My Giraffe

My giraffe has a neck as long as a broom handle.
His small head is as round as a football.
Eyelashes flicking like a fan.
His legs are as thin as pins.
Ears as smooth as silk.

Asma Aboobacker (11)
Frith Manor Primary School, Lullington Garth

Silver Gun

Ooh! Silver, silver, silver gun,
When will I touch you?
Ooh! Silver, silver, silver gun,
When will I use you?
Ooh! Silver, silver, silver gun,
You shoot like a rocket and blow like a torpedo.
Ooh! Silver, silver, silver gun,
I win you again for the thousandth time in our life.
Silver gun, kill him,
Silver gun, blow him,
Silver gun, put him in the graveyard.
Put your army on the warriors head and say
Ooh! Baddy me,
Ooh! Baddy me,
Silver gun.

Seremaia Malawakula (10)
Frith Manor Primary School, Lullington Garth

I Saw . . .

I saw a ferocious whirlwind palleting down on the city,
I saw a powerful lightning spinning in the sky,
I saw graceful snowflakes penetrating the midnight towers,
I saw the first drops of rain dancing merrily in the winter,
I saw the gleaming sun cascading down,
I saw the cracks of an earthquake making a warm, twilight blaze,
I saw a distended tornado branching its way into the tarmac,
I saw the heavy floods shooting objects into the sky.

James Soo (10)
Frith Manor Primary School, Lullington Garth

The Moonlit Beach

I adore the sight of the full moon
when it lies in its black blanket
in the sky.
I savour the sight of the stars
as they surround the white moon
completing the perfect picture.
I cherish the smooth texture of the
soft sand as it runs through
my fingers.
I value the peace that is brought
when I listen to the waves gently
breaking on the shore.
I truly love the calm sensation that sweeps
over me as I stand alone on the
beach, enchanted by the sea.
I wish I could capture the beauty of
the beach, so I could treasure it
forever.

Nicole Benghiat (10)
Frith Manor Primary School, Lullington Garth

Sunset

Etched against the blood-red skyline
I desire to see the fiery sun
As it brims over the edge of the horizon.
My heart seems engulfed in the flames of the sky
I treasure its overwhelming beauty
As it drowns me in its brilliant colours.
I wish that, if only, I could snatch the sunset
And take it home to share the magic with my family.

Alexandra Luke (10)
Frith Manor Primary School, Lullington Garth

I Saw A Dragon

I saw a dragon all red and orange,
I saw a house as big as a tree,
I saw the sun hotter than ever,
I saw an oak tree walking on the ground,
I saw a basket as big as me,
I saw a pink pig as big as a car,
I saw an orange leaf smiling happily,
I saw a blue teddy dancing with the sea,
I saw a bold letter jumping up and down,
I saw the clear river hitting his head upon the rocks,
I saw a thick book standing proudly on its shelf,
I saw a bright pink and red ball falling from the sky,
I saw a small boat swimming in the air,
I saw a fan blowing everyone away.

Romilia Antonio (10)
Frith Manor Primary School, Lullington Garth

The Lake

Ripples wandering around the lake,
Its shining blue surface, as smooth as a cake.
The lake is a thing of immeasurable beauty,
It's of humungous size - an infinity.

The sun gleamed down on the enchanting surface,
Seeming to send down floating gold bars as slow as a tortoise.
Surrounded by the forest green,
It's the most beautiful thing ever to be seen.

Few ever come here,
Nay, it is not their fear.
'Tis the fact that naught know of this place,
It really is a shame that none can see it - to me a pure disgrace.

Ameya Tripathi (11)
Frith Manor Primary School, Lullington Garth

Nobody Knows

As I look around the rocky playground,
All my eyes can see,
Is people laughing, saying,
'Brown boy, brown boy, get away from me.'
They spit on my shoes
And they put me in the blues,
They punch and they kick,
It makes me so sick,
My teacher does not know,
I'm trying to stay low.

I can't tell my family,
Or I will face the death penalty,
They won't let me go,
I sway in pain to and fro,
I'm trapped in a cage,
Filled with rage,
All I can do is write out this rhyme,
I will not forget this till the end of time.

Sagar Bhardwaj (11)
Frith Manor Primary School, Lullington Garth

Silverback

My great monkey swings like a jet through the thin air.
His lovely coat feels as if I am touching a smooth piece of hair.
He comes as fast as a speeding bullet.
He's scary when he is mad,
Like a raging tornado in the night sky.
He eats like a hungry giant ready for food.

Michael Csapo (11)
Frith Manor Primary School, Lullington Garth

A Kitten Likes . . .

I would love to taste a bowl of white, cool milk
As it lies silent and still in a round bowl.

I would dream of seeing a gigantic ball of wool
Swaying from side to side, tempting me.

I would be delighted to hear my owner
Tearing a packet of my favourite, tantalising treats.

I would enjoy the smell of fresh-cut, green grass
As I jauntily stalk the garden birds.

I would treasure feeling my owner's soft hand
Massaging my arched back.

Hana Namjou (10)
Frith Manor Primary School, Lullington Garth

Star

It dances through the velvet sky
It bursts out with rage with no might at all
It gleams in the ebony sky with the moon
It stands tall in its place
But if it gets angry it won't hold back
It fills up with rage and sends out bright flashes
The whole sky erupts with light
It shows strength
Eventually disappearing into the night sky.

Sawan Patel (10)
Frith Manor Primary School, Lullington Garth

I'd Rather Be

I'd rather be a hammer than a nail
I'd rather be a bird than a snail
I'd rather be a boat than a sail

I'd rather be the land than the sea
I'd rather be the hive than the bee
I'd rather be a leaf than a tree

I'd rather be a stream than a lake
I'd rather be the snow than the flake
I'd rather be the barbecue than the steak

I'd rather be the toaster than the bun
I'd rather be the moon than the sun
I'd rather be clever than dumb

I'd rather be a hammer than a nail
I'd rather be a bird than a snail
I'd rather be a boat than a sail

I'd rather be a land than the sea
I'd rather be a hive than a bee
I'd rather be a leaf than a stick.

Piers Tang (11)
Frith Manor Primary School, Lullington Garth

I Saw . . .

I saw a golden light as big as it could be.
I saw a puffy cloud shattering everything we could see.
I saw an earthquake spinning as fast as it could.
I saw a wild tornado crashing down and down.
I saw a mad rockslide crumbling down on me.
I saw a massive tree with rotten, brown leaves.

Rahul Saili (11)
Frith Manor Primary School, Lullington Garth

Alone

Alone.
Unwanted.
Different.
I lie helplessly on the ground,
My clothes torn and purple bruises
Covering my shivering body.
I feel numb.
I hear the laughter and giggling
As they run away,
Leaving me all alone.
I feel small and defenceless,
Like an animal in a cage.
One of me, four of them.
Nothing will ever change.
Only one thing matters . . .
Race.

Gabriela Wolfman (11)
Frith Manor Primary School, Lullington Garth

The Sea

Waves, wandering through the sea,
Stroking and sand like a gigantic hand,
Rippling gently onto the shore,
Washing away pebbles and shells,
Crashing against the white, stone cliffs,
The tide slowly covers the beach in a sheet of blue,
Golden sand, swimming in the gentle water,
Water seeping into the rigid rock caves,
Fish swimming in the splish-splashing sea,
Crabs scampering through the soft sand.

Chloe Lloyd-Jones (11)
Frith Manor Primary School, Lullington Garth

Spooky Poem!

When the moon takes the place of the sun
And suddenly light turns into dark
You feel like you are the only one
Who heard the dark spirit's hound bark.

Suddenly you are plunged into darkness
And your body is disabled with fear
Then your mind must confess
That you are scared over here.

Then a ghost walks past you
Followed by a couple of ghouls
After you see some men who
Had in their life been fools.

You hear a banshee screech
And feel the nightmare's wrath
You are now within evil's reach
And you feel as if you are a half.

Then the reaper slashes your soul
You have been murdered by a killer
Now you are not whole
As you have been a victim for the thriller.

Kamran Tajbakhsh (11)
Frith Manor Primary School, Lullington Garth

Destiny

My destiny is hidden behind the horizon
I may only touch it when I reach the future
It lies there where lights touch the sky
Where love rests uncaptured.

Clara-Laeila Laupette (9)
Frith Manor Primary School, Lullington Garth

Star

She trips and skips
She swoops and glides
Spreading golden dust
Across the gently snoozing world

Dancing with grace
And feet that never touch the floor
The moon is watching
He comes to join the dance

She sees no danger
Hears no sound
Feels with no feelings
Smells no fear

She trips and skips
She swoops and glides
Spreading golden dust
Across the gently snoozing world
    All in the mind of a shooting star.

Martha Gusack Limburg (11)
Frith Manor Primary School, Lullington Garth

Surreal Safari

I saw the half-bitten moon dangling in the sky,
I saw the majestic mountains drowning in the tears of clouds,
I saw the hands of the trees that follow the way of the midnight wind,
I saw the everlasting river cutting into the open rocks,
I saw the sun beating the early morning darkness,
I saw a jeep race out of the safari,
I saw the vile mud that stole my property,
I saw the man who saw this all behind an opaque door.

Diven Ganguly (11)
Frith Manor Primary School, Lullington Garth

Your Koala Baby

Never leave your koala baby,
Eating its leaf lunch,
A lion might come and eat it,
Crunch! Crunch! Crunch!

Never leave your koala baby,
Alone while having a nap,
A crocodile might come along,
Snap! Snap! Snap!

Never leave your koala baby,
Sitting in a bush,
Somebody might step on it,
Mush! Mush! Mush!

Always keep your koala baby,
As close as can be,
Then you'll both be safe,
A happy family!

Urshla Shah (10)
Frith Manor Primary School, Lullington Garth

A Barbecue

I saw the big, grey puff of smoke,
Floating in the wind.
I heard the sizzling of the fresh cooked meat,
Come to my ear in a shot.
I tasted the juicy steak,
With a sprinkle of salt and lemon.
I felt the grey steam from my meal,
Rise up into my dry face, now wet.
I smelt the freshly cooked aroma,
As it cooked on the brand new coloured grill.

Athos Kyriacou (10)
Frith Manor Primary School, Lullington Garth

I Saw . . .

I saw a hairy elephant telling lies
I saw an ant so small with big, wide eyes
I saw a flat snail licking my knees
I saw an oak tree dancing in the breeze
I saw a seahorse in the air
I saw a tall, skinny chair saying, 'Nearly there'
I saw a big fat whale hugging a bird
I saw a boy running from a beautiful girl
I saw a long horse keeping his hands and feet still
I saw a short dog with gills
I saw a pink flower singing out loud
I saw a big book feeling proud.

Fathiya Askar (10)
Frith Manor Primary School, Lullington Garth

Moonlight Memories

I saw the gleaming lake ripple as it swept across the shore,
I saw a blanket of flowers dancing in the moonlight,
I saw a glowing moon create a path of silver rays,
I saw the mysterious trees waving at their shadows,
I saw the blacked out sky keeping us cosy and warm,
I saw the luscious green grass swaying in the cool midnight breeze,
I saw the rocky, rugged rocks sitting like an Oompa Loompa,
I saw the round Earth like a large Jaffa cake,
I am the homeless child who saw it all.

Kayla Izikowitz (10)
Frith Manor Primary School, Lullington Garth

Night

The moon is bright
In the velvet black sky
It's well before
The morning is nigh.

The stars twinkle
And shine with delight
In the mist
Of the night.

The trees are swaying
Dancing with stars and moon
As the majestic wind
Hums her tune.

The misty fog covers the land
The cold air bites my cheeks
This scene is magical
So mystical, I could stand here for weeks.

The silver rays from the moon
In the pitch-black sky
My foggy breath covers my face
As I let out a sigh.

I can't believe that it's real
The face of the moon
Then as if by magic, it disappears
But I hope I see it soon!

Zehrah Hasan (10)
Frith Manor Primary School, Lullington Garth

Walking In The Park

The blackbirds sang their gentle song
The grass swayed from side to side
The flowers rocked on the mud's soft knee
The sun scorched my back as I lay on the grass
The spider injected me with its poisonous bite.

Benjamin Howard (10)
Frith Manor Primary School, Lullington Garth

Moving Through The Day

Rising high,
Finding its spot,
Making its light,
So night has stopped,
Waking us up.
To start the day,
Moving slowly,
Reaching midday.

Bright in the sky,
The sun hovers brightly,
Flashing sunrays,
And heating us tightly,
Finding its way,
Through the sky,
Overtaking midday,
Night's gone - bye-bye!

The sun in the west,
Sets with yellow and red,
Silhouetted trees shadow,
I observe from my bed,
The sun is beautiful,
Soft music plays,
The end of the evening,
It's the end of today.

Toby Norman (10)
Frith Manor Primary School, Lullington Garth

I Saw The Seaside

I saw the glistening sand sparkling like gold glitter.
I saw the seashells scattered around the beach.
I saw the yellow sun gleaming in the clear blue sky.
I saw the calm sea still as still.
I saw the seaweed wiggle in the water.
I saw the pier taking the people across the sea.

Daniel Kravetz (10)
Frith Manor Primary School, Lullington Garth

Dog Fight!

Growling angrily at the stranger,
My adorable dog, Chocolate,
Knew the stranger was a danger.
Lifting his paws,
Sharpening his claws,
Chocolate got ready to fight.
He gave the stranger a gigantic bite
And rolled across the ground,
Turning round and round and round.
Getting dizzy as they spin,
Knocking into a thousand bins,
Finally Chocolate stopped for a rest,
He didn't win, but tried his best.
Left the stranger well alone
And crawled to his bowl where he gnawed his bone.
And the stranger - oh!
He went back home!

Carmen Tam (10)
Frith Manor Primary School, Lullington Garth

Fearsome Forest

I saw the pitch-black sky blinding the Earth
I saw the great grey wolves howling at the glowing moon
                                in their soaked coats of fur
I saw the forest trees creaking in the mist
I saw a crowd of bears catching salmon from the waterfall
I saw the owls with their glowing eyes fade into the darkness
I saw the rain flooding the earth
I saw the creatures big and small crawling on the trees and floor
I saw myself see all this.

Riyad Ebrahim (10)
Frith Manor Primary School, Lullington Garth

The Lady Down The Street

Have you met the lady
Living down the street?
She plays such gentle music
So soft and sweet.

Her harp sings so beautifully
When she is sad, oh how it cries
She gives advice to all
Her words are so very wise.

She wears silky clothes
She smells of aromatic spice
She ties back her hair with flowers
All pretty and nice.

She is never lonely
As she is everybody's friend
The children always visit her
For her smile won't end.

Robyn Wase (11)
Frith Manor Primary School, Lullington Garth

I'd Rather . . .

I'd rather be happy than sad
I'd rather be good than bad
I'd rather be sane than mad
I'd rather be a child than a dad.

I'd rather be young than old
I'd rather be hot than cold
I'd rather do as I want than be told
I'd rather be kept than sold.

I'd rather have less than more
I'd rather be eleven than four
I'd rather be interesting than a bore
I'd rather have peace than war.

Anoushka Amin (11)
Frith Manor Primary School, Lullington Garth

Life Is A . . .

Life is a roller coaster
You have your ups and downs
We are the track
You are the passengers
We take you on the ride of life.

Life is a merry-go-round
You go round in circles
We are the horses
You go at such speed
We take you on the ride of life.

Life is a ghost train
You get a fright
We are the guiding carriages
Showing you the way
We take you on the ride of life.

Life is a big wheel
It takes its time
We are the poles
We hold you in a safe place
We take you on the ride of life.

Life is a circus
You have your laughs
We are the clowns
To make sure you smile
We take you on the ride of life.

Life has an ending
You don't know when it comes
We are the gates that close it
It might take you by surprise
We take you on the ride of life.

Mona Tank (11)
Frith Manor Primary School, Lullington Garth

Chocolate Cake

The smell pervades the house,
I become irresistible.
I creep down the stairs with my eyes closed
And my nose in the air.
The chocolate cake awaits me.
I grasp the fridge handle
And it opens automatically.
There it is!
I tentatively carry it out of the fridge,
Looking at it maliciously
And licking my lips.
Slurp!
Suddenly it's all gone!
My belly aches,
I feel sick.

Bianca Boyce Zuccotto (11)
Frith Manor Primary School, Lullington Garth

Midnight Garden

I saw the pitch-black sky protecting us below
I saw the glowing moon getting bitten by the clouds
I saw the silhouette of the branches viciously waving their
skeletal fingers at me
I saw the emerald-green grass waving from side to side
I saw the glittering stars hiding behind the clouds
I saw the chocolate-brown fences getting hit by the wind
I saw the sleeping rose getting hit by the wind.

Michael Kleopa (10)
Frith Manor Primary School, Lullington Garth

Shadows Of Hell

The crimson sun is setting
And the moonlit darkness appears,
Stars of heaven shine brightly
And so darkness is found.

Suddenly shadows appear
And creatures step out of a mist,
The reign of chaos is here
And evil is here to assist.

Ghosts and ghouls descend from thin air,
Feeding on death and fear,
Every step you take, you must take care,
As danger lurks around here.

Dev Dhokia (11)
Frith Manor Primary School, Lullington Garth

Sapphire Dolphin

Sleek and silent he dives beneath the sea,
What can this mysterious animal be?
His smooth, silk body with a silver hue,
Gliding, twirling right through.

Seeking and hunting, looking for fish,
What a yummy, delicious dish.
Dancing, swirling in the moonlit sky,
Leaping, looking like he can fly!

Alexandra Van Colle (11)
Frith Manor Primary School, Lullington Garth

I'd Love To Be An Eagle

I'd love to see my prey down below me,
As I fly above treetops.
I dream to hear the scream of myself,
Proving that I am the boss.
I'd adore the touch of thermals in the morning,
As the warm air lifts me up.
I'd love to smell my prey's fear,
As it cowers away in the corner.
I'd enjoy the taste of fresh water,
Cascading over a waterfall.
I'd love to feel the power of my wings,
Beating the air around me.
I'd love to be an eagle -
The almighty bird.

Joshua Ferrol (10)
Frith Manor Primary School, Lullington Garth

A Sunset In The Garden

I saw the orange, hot sun peeping out of the white, fluffy clouds
I saw the golden-red leaves floating down to the ground
I saw the blue, sparkly pond glistening under the sun
I saw the green blades of grass huddling together
I saw the hard, brown earth providing homes for the creatures
I saw the branches of the leaves dancing to the breeze
I saw the small tulips kissing the air
I saw the blue, bright sky shining down on me with glee.

Lisa Graham (10)
Frith Manor Primary School, Lullington Garth

Shooting Star

I said bye to my family
And got ready to set off.
My legs and arms burning,
My whole body went bright red hot.

My body rumbled like a rocket,
Waiting to go off.
10, 9, 8, 7, 6, 5 . . .
Closing my eyes I waited to rise,
High up into the air.

. . . 4, 3, 2, 1,
I rocketed into the sky,
Leaving my family behind,
My body on fire.

Rise, rise, rise,
I summoned my body to go higher.
Soon enough I saw the towns,
Glimmering like a diamond.

Glitter trailing behind me,
I soared through the misty clouds,
Twisting and turning my body,
Decorating the jet-black sky.

I sped above colourful countries,
I towered over raging cliffs,
I zigzagged through the everlasting clouds,
Performing acrobatic tricks.

My powers are diminished,
My light is growing faint,
My destiny fulfilled,
I finally blow, spreading pastel paint.

Owen Baxter (10)
Frith Manor Primary School, Lullington Garth

Have You Done It Yet?

Have you done your homework?
Have you done it yet?
Have you neatly made your bed?
Your friends are coming over - Tom, Tim and Ted.

You have to get the shopping,
You have to buy the milk.
You must get the food for lunch,
Quick, quick, quick!

You have to clean the kitchen,
Tidy up that design set!
You have to cook the dinner,
Have you done it yet?

Emilie Wolfman (9)
Frith Manor Primary School, Lullington Garth

The Panda

I saw a little panda,
He was small and sweet.
He was quite plump,
For he'd had a lot to eat.

His fur was nice and soft,
It was black and white.
He was very cute,
And a lovely sight.

He chomped his stalk of bamboo,
Munch, munch, munch.
Now it's all gone,
Crunch, crunch, crunch.

Alisha Amin (8)
Frith Manor Primary School, Lullington Garth

Crying

Tears run down my swollen cheek,
Why does the world seem so bleak?

There it goes! Fast! So quick!
They make a sound, drip, drip and drip.

Suddenly my cheeks flush red,
I want to go home, to my bed.

I have to remember those cheerful times,
When we were happy - sang funny rhymes.

But now it is the end,
I have no one to be my friend.

But what's this? Can it be real?
Finally someone understands just how I feel.

Maya Benson (9)
Frith Manor Primary School, Lullington Garth

Chocolate

I love to eat chocolate, so creamy and sweet,
But when it is melted, it's not such a treat.
Milk chocolate is my favourite, I eat it day and night,
But if someone takes my chocolate away from me,
I'll start a fight.

I love to eat chocolate, so creamy and sweet,
And chocolate is what I love to eat.
But chocolate is perfect.

Robert White (8)
Frith Manor Primary School, Lullington Garth

Little Baby Tiger

Cute, cuddly,
Soft and warm,
Prowling in the jungle,
Claws as sharp as horns.

Following his mummy,
Down the refreshing stream,
His coat is like a stripy scarf,
Flowing in the windy draft.

Playing with his mummy,
In the warm stream,
Splashing and rolling,
Like he's in a dream.

Frederyka Rolle (8)
Frith Manor Primary School, Lullington Garth

Flowers

A tulip is nice and bright,
A daisy is snow-white.
A sunflower grows high,
Almost as big as the sky.
A crocus is very small,
The opposite to daffodils, which are tall.
Fuchsias are light,
They are such a pretty sight.

Jessica Benghiat (8)
Frith Manor Primary School, Lullington Garth

The Cloud Dragon

It is a lazy summer's day,
I lie on my sweaty back and stare at the shapes in the sky,
                                    known as clouds.
The famous cloud dragon, floats in front of me . . .
His fierce, pouchy eyes glow, as if bright red!
His fluffy snout, ends in two flaming, white nostrils,
His ears are pricked, his whole image floating motionlessly
                                    in the periwinkle sky.
The dragon's scaly, bumpy, arched back, finishes in a spiked,
                                    wavy tail.
He bares his enormous, inflated fangs towards me, as though
                                    he is angry.
I feel scared and uncomfortable - is it me he is envying?
But now, he spreads his cream, woolly wings and fades away,
                                    slowly, slowly . . .
No one ever knows where he will appear next,
Maybe he will hover over your front door - who knows?

Annie Maddison (10)
Frith Manor Primary School, Lullington Garth

I Saw . . .

I saw the colourful blooms in the sunlight
I saw the wet grass dry in the heat
I saw the fiery sun warm the world
I saw the tall tree wave in the wind
I saw a red apple drop to the ground
I saw the creatures of the morning gather their breakfast
I saw the hovering clouds move unwillingly
I saw the barred gate imprisoning us.

Nicola Bullivant (10)
Frith Manor Primary School, Lullington Garth

Clouds

I stare up to the clear blue sky,
Watching clouds drift lazily by.
Shapes form, all different kinds,
At strange, unexpected times.

I slowly drift into a cloudy dream,
Ponies and bears painted cream.
A fierce dragon with fiery flames,
A pride of lions with rainbow-coloured manes.

A tortoise racing a slimy snail,
A cat perched on a window sill.
A pig dancing on a country lane
And puffs of smoke out of the old steam train.

I suddenly awake.

I find myself looking into the sky again.
Then I can finally make,
A portrait of me,
With all the imagination it will take.

Su Ling Yeoh (10)
Frith Manor Primary School, Lullington Garth

Puffins

Three little puffins were partial to muffins,
They couldn't be parted from muffins,
They were coughing and puffing all day long.
One puffin ate handful of muffins
And all of the puffins were fluffy.

Roxanne Khalaj (9)
Frith Manor Primary School, Lullington Garth

My Magic, Secret Carpet

Who wants to ride on my magic carpet today
And visit exciting places in the way?
Let's fly high into the clouds,
Away from the traffic, away from the crowds.
Where shall we go first? Yes, I know,
Let's go see polar bears and play in the snow.

A *whoosh* and a *bump* and at last we've landed,
Where are we now? I hope we're not stranded!
We're in a desert with snakes and cacti,
I'm really thirsty, come on let's fly.

Now we're flying in the air,
A gust of wind takes us somewhere.
We seem to have landed, but we're still rather high,
Are we on a mountain or are we in the sky?
Underneath me is a rumble, I feel quite hot,
My feet start to tremble and my heart beats a lot!
We're on a volcano and I think I'm going to die!
Come on carpet, fly, fly, fly!

The carpet won't stop, it's out of control,
Up into space, we've gone through a black hole.
A crash, a bump, have we landed on Mars?
I'm looking around now, I see only stars.
This planet is so red, so dusty and scary,
What's down that crater? Aahh, an alien so hairy!
I hate this place, I think I should go,
Phew! I'm back on Earth now, right down below!

I'm in my bedroom, carpet on the floor,
Mum comes in and opens the door.
'What's on the carpet, sand, grit and snow?
How did it get there?'
She'll never know!

Amy Parkin (10)
Frith Manor Primary School, Lullington Garth

Dancing Dolphins

Looking at dancing dolphins,
Spinning and swirling like the wind,
Watch them flapping their fabulous fins,
Just like a grand fan!

They are such extraordinary creatures,
That I need to take a picture,
See that big, beautiful blue one?
Quick, take a photo, *click, click!*

They are so splendid,
I wish I could ride on one,
I jump into the emerald-green sea
And there they are . . .

Dancing dolphins, waiting for me!
I hop on one
And we swim away,
This is the greatest and most magical day ever!

Nikita Mittman (9)
Frith Manor Primary School, Lullington Garth

Spelling

I've mastered all my spelling words,
I've really had enough,
These words are far too easy,
Like *sought* and *drought* and *trough*.

I've mastered all my spelling words,
Like *sighted, freight* and *slight*,
I checked my answers with *thorough* care,
I've grown to a tremendous *height*.

I've mastered all my spelling words,
I'm glad to be alive,
Oops! One more word, that's *partially*,
But I learnt it when I was five!

Jonathan Clingman (8)
Frith Manor Primary School, Lullington Garth

My Family

My mum
She is Santa Claus,
Always giving me presents.
She is my bank,
Giving me extra money.
She is my taxi,
Taking me everywhere.
She is the sun,
Wrapping her rays around me.

My dad
He is a book,
Full of wonderful words.
He is a post box,
Always receiving letters.
He is a bulldozer,
Picking me up from school.
He is a moon,
Shining through the night.

My sister
She is Harry Potter,
Brave and loyal.
She is a pillow,
Soft and cuddly.
She is a princess,
Beautiful and kind.
She is a star,
Twinkling and dancing around.

Diana Grant-Davie (9)
Frith Manor Primary School, Lullington Garth

Cat

They call me Ginger, but really I'm tabby.
They feed me salmon, but I like tuna.
My bed is a basket, but I would like a cushion.
They gave me a fake mouse to play with,
But really I would prefer a ball of string.
They stroke me under the chin, but I feel ticklish there.
I want to be with my mum, but I can't find her.
I am very lonely as there's no one like me to play with.
I wish they could understand how I want things to be.

But what's this?
Two blue eyes looking down at me!
Two pointy ears as tall as mountains!
One pink, soft tongue trying to lick me!
It's a friend at last!
Come play with me!

Sehel Khandwala (8)
Frith Manor Primary School, Lullington Garth

Ripple

Swirling, twirling, going quiet,
Everything is calm, no riot!
Fish come swimming, thinking it is food,
What a surprise they get when it's not!
First starts little, then gets big,
Swirling, twirling like a Catherine wheel,
Only not loud, but it feels like a hard puzzle,
A mystery trying to be solved!
Swirling, twirling round and round,
The prettiest pattern I've ever found!
Swirly, swirling, twirly, twirling,
All started from a plop!
Smaller, bigger, a pretty figure,
Swirling, twirling, stop.

Ruby Stolerman (9)
Frith Manor Primary School, Lullington Garth

You Are Like The Sun To Me

You are like the sun to me,
Always cheerful whatever the case.
You are like the sun to me,
Always happy wherever the place.
You are like the sun to me,
Always thoughtful when people are down.
You are like the sun to me,
Always comforting when you're wearing a frown.
You are like the sun to me,
Always bright.
You are like the sun to me,
You would never start a fight.
You are like the sun to me,
Always loving and life-giving, I can guarantee that.
You are like the sun to me,
I wish I was the same to you.
You are my friend and I wish I could do the same back.

Kimon Demetriou (10)
Frith Manor Primary School, Lullington Garth

A Barbecue With My Friends

As I walked into the garden
I saw the fire glowing as I put the meat in.
I smelt the nice fire roasting the meat.
I heard the fire cracking and popping.
I felt the nice heat blowing on me.
Then I stuck my teeth into the nice, succulent piece of meat.

Hamza Mushtaq (11)
Frith Manor Primary School, Lullington Garth

The Battle

The sky is dark and the ground is red
As the cold metal weapon landed on the warrior's head.

'Alas,' he said, 'all my army is dead
Nothing can I do to keep me from my doom.'

There was a dim light shining on the injured knight as he
Lay in fright.

Then a shout
And a crush a great hush and darkness clouded them all.

All was quiet, until he heard a great riot.
He saw his family once again.

Cameron Clark (10)
Frith Manor Primary School, Lullington Garth

Fireworks Night

Glittering sparks of every colour, red, green, orange, blue,
Whee! Off into the air!
Little children run around excitedly, clutching sparkling sparklers,
Bang! A blinding flash of white light exploded in the night sky,
Hands are warmed by the flickering fire, the flames dancing around,
Mocking me.
Merriment spreading through me, like a colourful rainbow spreading
Through the sky.
I watch this amazing display while clutching my mum's warm and
Comforting hand.
The aroma of beefburgers wafts through my nostrils, I feel happy.

Shi Wan Chu (10)
Frith Manor Primary School, Lullington Garth

Raindrop

I
am a
raindrop!
I am very upset.
Why does everyone
run away from me when
I drop from the sky to pay them
a visit? I don't want to harm them
I just want to be their friend. I am
a raindrop. I am very upset.
Why does everyone run
and jump on me when
I fall to the ground?
I am a raindrop.
I am very
upset.

Kyla Lief (9)
Frith Manor Primary School, Lullington Garth

A Barbecue With My Friends

I saw delicious, sizzling sausages and lovely brown bacon,
I heard my friends talking happily and lively,
I tasted the smoke from the hot fire,
I felt the excitement of tasting the delicious food,
I smelt the scent of the irresistible barbecue food.

Adrian Wong (10)
Frith Manor Primary School, Lullington Garth

Lonely Girl

Her lips, red rubies glistening gracefully in the sunlight
Wisps of hair rest on her shoulders breathing in the fresh air
A colour so bright it blinds the sun as it smiles down at her
Crystal-blue eyes stare constantly at the flowing lagoon waters
She lifts up her head, revealing her pale, white face to the world
                                                            outside

Cheekbones tense, gritting her teeth
Her ears covered in sparkling, silver rings
Her nose swollen with the colours of the rainbow from recent
                                                    happenings

She is alone
Tempted to run away or disappear into a small dot
Getting smaller and smaller
She can't though, she has to stay
She can't leave now
No, not now.

Katy Wilkinson (11)
Frith Manor Primary School, Lullington Garth

I Saw A . . .

I saw a lion with a drooping nose as long as a branch of a tree,
I saw a chicken with knives for eyes,
I saw a football trembling with fear,
I saw a tennis ball behind broken glass,
I saw an ant swallow up a whale in a sea brim full of ginger ale.

I saw a pismire lift an elephant,
I saw a fabulous fly that could never die,
I saw a bird that could not fly,
I saw a door that led me to Heaven.

Kishen Dhokia (10)
Frith Manor Primary School, Lullington Garth

The Moon

Creeping quietly through the town,
Not a sound can be heard.
In the middle of the night
The moon appears to be dancing along
The silvery midnight sky.
A rustle of the leaves
In the oak trees nearby,
The dogs in their kennels,
The cats in their beds,
Everyone asleep.
Nothing can break the silence now.
A mouse running through the park
Alerting danger, for a dog is awake.
The silence has broken with its piercing barks,
Park creatures try to settle down,
All is quiet, silence returns.
Dawn breaks,
The moon's asleep,
Night is over,
For now.

Giorgia Ferri (10)
Frith Manor Primary School, Lullington Garth

Autumn

Autumn days are long and misty,
Leaves falling, getting crispy.

The sky is darkening, back to schools,
Lots of new teachers, plenty of rules.

The summer birds have flown away,
And left their nests today.

The countryside is quiet and plain,
All the time it seems to rain.

Naomi Warrenberg (9)
Frith Manor Primary School, Lullington Garth

Sunset

I see her, the blazing beach ball,
Start to fall,
I see her, there in the great waters,
Bobbing up and down,
I see her show her last fading lights,
Orange, pink, blue, green,
I see her sink under the water,
Her head popping up now and then,
I see her, lights still showing,
Leaving the clouds pink and orange,
I see her show her last strand of fiery hair,
Leaving me alone,
I see her friend take her place,
The glowing silver ball,
I see the sun's friend call the stars,
To brighten up the inky, black night,
I'll see her tomorrow,
After her rest.

Maya Saravan-Butler (10)
Frith Manor Primary School, Lullington Garth

I'd Rather . . .

I'd rather be a window than a windowpane,
I'd rather be the sun than the rain,
I'd rather be a dog than a fish,
I'd rather be a fork than a dish,
I'd rather be a book than a hook,
I'd rather be a tree than sit on your knee,
I'd rather sing than be a king,
I'd rather be a pen than a hen,
I'd rather be a mum than a nun,
I'd rather be a toy than a boy,
I'd rather have joy than annoy.

Vasiliana Onoufriou (11)
Frith Manor Primary School, Lullington Garth

Flickery Flames

The flickery flames jumping up and down
Try to escape from the cold, quiet house
They leap up the ancient chimney
And glare at me as if I'm keeping a torturer
Trapped in the fireplace
Wanting a key to come and let them out.

Suddenly a flick of its skin leaps away
As it lands it becomes a ball, like the sun
Spreading around, teasing me
I reach the door, wheezing and coughing
My home is lost - I have nothing now!

Victoria Matthews (10)
Frith Manor Primary School, Lullington Garth

The Sea

Watching with its dark blue eyes,
Feeling feet on its soft, gold sand.
As it swims up to cover the rocks,
The waves trickle round and round.
The fish tickle it while they swim on its body,
It sees entertainment on the beach.
It flounces in - a Flamenco dancer!
And hits me - hard!
The castanets clap,
The sea leaves the stage -
Performance over - mission complete!

Sophia Tanner (10)
Frith Manor Primary School, Lullington Garth

Lion

Prowling, purring through the jungle,
With a smile upon her brow,
In her coat of golden sunlight,
Dancing with delight across the plain,
She pounces on the terrified deer
And with silver paws, glinting in the moonlight,
Feasts upon her prey
And she drags her slain foe,
As fast as lightning across the plain,
To where the ravenous pack are waiting.

Samuel Ehrenstein (10)
Frith Manor Primary School, Lullington Garth

A Barbecue With Friends

I saw the tasty-looking sausages
Toasting on the fire-hot barbecue.

I heard the sizzling of the meaty burgers
Burning to death.

I felt the cold lemonade
Rush through my dry mouth.

I smelt the cold tomato ketchup
On top of my hot dog.

Albie Bigland (10)
Frith Manor Primary School, Lullington Garth

The Green Knight

Deep in Castle Green Skull,
In the cold and mould where only doctors go,
There is the most horrid monster thinkable -
The green knight,
He is always low.
He coughs and he sneezes
And he never eases,
But still he wears his armour.
His doctors treat him with lots of medicine
To make him calmer,
The only problem is,
They can't get through his pyjamas.
He punches and he kicks,
He even hits with sticks,
But he never ends his traumas.
If we ever go near him,
His only remark is to harm us.
When you touch his skin,
It's as cold as ice.
He's always so ill now,
Nothing comes near him,
Not even lice.
Then a miracle happened,
He got well!
But still his face is a shade of green.
So now he is the best knight alive
Because everyone is sick
When he appears on the scene!

Robbie Davies (11)
Frith Manor Primary School, Lullington Garth

I'd Rather Be . . .

I'd rather be alive than dead,
I'd rather be a lady than a man,
I'd rather be a winner than a loser,
I'd rather be brave than scared,
I'd rather have blue eyes than purple eyes,
I'd rather go to school than be a fool,
I'd rather be nice than bad,
I'd rather be me than you.

Riddhi Soni (10)
Frith Manor Primary School, Lullington Garth

There Was A Girl Called Kelly . . .

There was a girl called Kelly
Who ate a lot of red jelly
She was the host
Who had the most
That girl had a fat belly.

Mehmet Doldur (8)
Grazebrook Primary School, Stoke Newington

Pigs

The Black Jupiter pigs
Who love yellow wigs
Have wonderful trotters
That turned into potters
And the only cure was figs.

Joseph Tollington (8)
Grazebrook Primary School, Stoke Newington

The Hole

A hole doesn't give a welcome to me,
It's dark when you're looking down a hole, you see.
When you're looking down it
Your happiness drains
What could be down there?
Guts? Or brains?
Could it be monsters?
Or people dying?
Maybe they're alive
But only lying
Wait, I feel stupid to think of this
It's an empty hole, of course it is
I'll walk away from this
That's what I'll do
Wait!
What was that growl?
Was it you?

Jack Mayer (9)
Grazebrook Primary School, Stoke Newington

Boys And Girls

There was a man called Nelly
And there was a girl called Kelly
They went to the park
To see a shark
And then they found a penny.

Tianna Morgan (7)
Grazebrook Primary School, Stoke Newington

Rhyming Colour

What is red?
A book is red, reading with me.

What is black?
My rubber is black, here with me in the sack.

What is white?
My clothes are white, sleeping with me in the night.

What is green?
An apple is green, saying hello to the queen.

What is yellow?
A leaf is yellow, standing still like a marshmallow.

What is pink?
A felt tip is pink, living in the kitchen wasting ink.

Nadeerah Esmail (9)
Grazebrook Primary School, Stoke Newington

Doug The Bug

Doug the bug
Met a plug
In the deep blue sea
Said Doug the bug
To the plug
'Would you like some tea?'

Doug the bug
Met the plug
In the BBC
Said Doug the bug
To the plug
'Why haven't you finished your tea?'

Douglas MacLeod (8)
Grazebrook Primary School, Stoke Newington

Monday's Child

Monday's child spins a web
Tuesday's child stays in bed
Wednesday's child likes to read a book
Thursday's child likes to look
Friday's child is loving and happy
Saturday's chid has to clean a nappy
But the child that's born on Sunday
Is very happy and likes to play.

Simbi Aileru (8)
Grazebrook Primary School, Stoke Newington

The Stinger

Triple stinger
White winger
Honeycomb clinger
Bee stinger
Sweet sucker
Spider plucker
Big striper
Hairy viper.

Emilio Masotti-Black (9)
Grazebrook Primary School, Stoke Newington

Big Red Nose

There was a man with a big red nose
As old as his 25th century clothes
Which made him sleepy
And he was very weepy
Just like a rose.

Christopher Strongman (7)
Grazebrook Primary School, Stoke Newington

Snow

Snowballs are big
Snowballs are small
Snowballs can be any size
You can chuck the snow
You can kick the snow
You can do lots of things with snow
Why don't you go and play with the snow?
Snow is a wonderful sight for people
What did I say?
You said *snow*.

Muhammed Akbulut (8)
Grazebrook Primary School, Stoke Newington

Monday's Child

Monday's child is very sneaky,
Tuesday's child is more than cheeky,
Wednesday's child likes to go out,
Thursday's child always freaks out,
Friday's child is very funny,
Saturday's child works hard for money,
But the child that is born on the Sabbath day,
Makes that day a happy day.

Mariam Balogun-Etti (8)
Grazebrook Primary School, Stoke Newington

The Rainbow Poem

Yellow is the sun, shining bright,
Blue is the dark, glowing in the night.
Green is the grass, blowing in the park,
Indigo are the sea animals, just like a shark.
Pink is the flamingo, dancing round like mad,
Orange is the orange, which always squirts a dad.

Renaye Roberts (9)
Grazebrook Primary School, Stoke Newington

The Fridge

Food, food, fish and chips,
Then I go and wash my hips.
Food, food, a pizza will be nice,
And I will have a nice cold ice.
In my freezer I will have some ice,
And it will be on my pizza, that's nice.
In my freezer I will have ice cream,
When I eat it, I'm going to scream.

Lavana Salton (9)
Grazebrook Primary School, Stoke Newington

Monday's Child

Monday's child is very nice,
Tuesday's child has lots of lice.
Wednesday's child is very thin,
Thursday's child stuck his head in a bin.
Friday's child is very thick,
Saturday's child gets a kick.
But the child born on Sunday,
Likes to say 'hey!'

Sam Apcar (8)
Grazebrook Primary School, Stoke Newington

Monday's Child

Monday's child is very cheeky,
Tuesday's child is very squeaky.
Wednesday's child is very funny,
Thursday's child is a bunny.
Friday's child is full of luck,
Saturday's child likes to suck.
But the child that is born on Sunday,
Likes to have a fun day.

Syedur Rahman (8)
Grazebrook Primary School, Stoke Newington

Sound Maker

Sound maker
Light giver
Video player
Remote control obeyer
Baby sitter
Entertainer
PS2 player
Pleasure giver
Brain washer.

Caspar Swindells (9)
Grazebrook Primary School, Stoke Newington

Cool Thing

Good shape
Has light
Fast runner
Four legger
Cool speed
Has doors
Very fast
Very cool
Very clean
Cool wheels.

Chadrick Bonnick (8)
Grazebrook Primary School, Stoke Newington

In The Wood

Molly liked peaches
But she hated leeches
She lived in a wood
Quite near Robin Hood
And did not like beaches.

Isobel McIntyre (7)
Grazebrook Primary School, Stoke Newington

Tutankhamen

4000 years in a tomb
surrounded by treasures
there lies a wrapped up mummy
waiting to be found
with a mask upon his face
four sunboats by his side
with writing on the walls
and paintings all around
he'll go off to the afterlife
where gods are standing by
and have a good time t here
and he'll never really die.

Claire Piper (8)
Grazebrook Primary School, Stoke Newington

Monday's Child

Monday's child likes to stay in bed,
  Tuesday's child likes to drive a ped.

Wednesday's child is lazy too,
  Thursday's child likes to put his head down the loo.

Friday's child screams and screams,
  Saturday's child likes to eat cream.

And the child that's born on Sunday,
  Likes to have a nice day.

Atilla Ardic (8)
Grazebrook Primary School, Stoke Newington

The Washing Machine

Round and round
Twisting and twirling
Like a coloured rainbow ball
Twisting and thrashing
Bashing and slashing
The metal of the machine
Like snakes coiling
Swirling and spinning
Tumbling, coiling and curling.

Micha Horgan (8)
Grazebrook Primary School, Stoke Newington

Books

In the world there are over 1,000,000 books.
Most aren't about the importance of looks.
My opinion of them is very clear,
The very good ones are not about beer,
Though some of them are about cooks.

Aidan Largin (8)
Grazebrook Primary School, Stoke Newington

The Funky Monkey

I know a monkey
Who is very funky
It likes eating pears
With the other bears
That's funky monkey.

Lauren Daly (8)
Grazebrook Primary School, Stoke Newington

Fast Thing

Good shape
Has lights
Fast runner
Four gears
Cool speed
Has doors
Has seats
Is cool
And clean
Has engine.

Kane Aves (8)
Grazebrook Primary School, Stoke Newington

Washing Machine Poem

Round and round and round it goes
Where it stops nobody knows
With its twisting and turning
Its spinning and swirling
It's the swashing washing machine.

Kieran Kirkwood (8)
Grazebrook Primary School, Stoke Newington

Cricket, Cricket

Cricket, cricket, hit the wicket
Cricket, cricket, bowl the ball
Cricket, cricket, hit the stumps
Cricket, cricket, watch them fall
Cricket, cricket, is so fun
Cricket, cricket, score a run
Cricket, cricket, at the end of the day
Cricket, cricket, it's fun to play.

Jordan Hanlon (9)
Jubilee Primary School, Stoke Newington

Endless Poem

Five men in a desert,
All around a camp fire.
The first man says,
'Someone tell a story.'
So the second man says,
'I will.' And this is how it went . . .

Five men in a desert,
All around a camp fire.
The first man says,
'Someone tell a story.'
So the second man says,
'I will.' And this is how it went . . .

Five men in a desert,
All around a camp fire.
The first man says,
'Someone tell a story.'
So the second man says,
'I will.' And this is how it went . . .

Alex Gibson (10)
Jubilee Primary School, Stoke Newington

Six Lights

One of six Lamonath lights each of the old races possessed.
The first of them sleeps deep in a dying dwarf king's chest,
Another held safe in the hand of an elven maiden,
The third is buried deep beneath the forest's hallowed glade,
The next is in the hands of men encased in magical sword,
A fifth is hidden unto the west over the great river's ford,
The last is lost beneath the waves, held by an evil race.
And if all these lights were brought together,
The undying darkness would show its twisted face.

Conor Litten Beatty (10)
Jubilee Primary School, Stoke Newington

Remembering The Park In Kosovo

There,
Where
The sun
Shines in the pond.
Here,
Only grey clouds
In the sky.

Then,
When
I was playing
With my friends in the park.
Now,
I miss my friends
So far away.

Now,
How
I feel a bit sad.
But I will get better
Because I have new friends.
Then,
I still remember
Kosovo.

Domjeta Baliu (8)
Jubilee Primary School, Stoke Newington

Friends

Who are they?
What do they do?
Do they help us?
Yes or no?

Can you trust them
With your secrets?
Do they help us?
Yes or no?

Carmelita Bennett (11)
Jubilee Primary School, Stoke Newington

In Me

In me there are
Blue frosted tears of rain
Splashing here, there and everywhere.

In me there is
A piece of music played
On the edge of a waterfall
Smoothing down
Out of nowhere.

In me there is
A butterfly dancing
Hovering
Thinking of nothing
But nightmares.

In me there is
A soft piece of cloth
As thin as floating
Ice on a pond
Just bobbing.

Charlotte Joseph (8)
Jubilee Primary School, Stoke Newington

Tornado

A tornado heading this way, smacking all creations.
Confusion in my mate's mind.
All that's on my mind is getting through here
Travelling across the world . . .
To my heavenly tasting sweets near my bubble bath
. . . in one place on my plate.

Aamenah Mulla (10)
Jubilee Primary School, Stoke Newington

Prejudice

People avoid me
I'm not part of the family
Even though it's sorrowful;
I don't belong with the crowd
I'm the ugly duckling
There's no comfort for me.

Tomorrow it will change
I will *comfort* everyone
They will *notice* me
They will come to *me*
I will give them hope
I'll fit in with them.

I'll be part of the family
Even though it's sorrowful.

I want everyone to see
I'm a person too.
We're all part of the world
We're all equal.

We're all part of the family
Even though it's sorrowful.

Bryher Litten Beatty (8)
Jubilee Primary School, Stoke Newington

Smelly Shelly

There was once a girl called Shelly
Who ate a whole plate of jelly
To school she tumbled
And her belly rumbled
And when she got home she was smelly.

Maariyah Dawood (9)
Jubilee Primary School, Stoke Newington

Remembering My Special Place - Kent

There,
Where
My favourite place
The glittering sea smashing on the rocks
Glistening in the sun.

Then,
When
The air is fresh
The dolphins swim
And the sun rises.
Now,
The air is full of smoke
And I miss Kent more than ever.

Now,
How
The birds in London do not sing at all
The sun does not
Shine.
Then,
I remember
Seagulls singing beautifully in my best place - Kent.

Dayna Wyatt (8)
Jubilee Primary School, Stoke Newington

You Don't Know Me

Listen to me, my name is Speedy,
I'll gun you down with my MC.
You don't know me,
I'll kill you, you see.
Man like me got stung by a bee,
Fell off a mountain, dropped in a sea.
You don't know me,
I'll chop up your beanie.

Junaid Vahed (11)
Jubilee Primary School, Stoke Newington

Remembering My Bedroom At Peace

Here,
Where
In my bedroom
With toys and soldiers everywhere
Everything to do in my bedroom.
There,
Mud, wet, here and there,
Nothing much but cloud.

Then,
When
I see the glittering day
When I look from my window
Every day.
Now,
The streets of noise and terror
Howling with dismay.

Now,
How
It's peaceful again,
Now I can get away,
Now I can play every day.
Then,
I still see terror in London
Howling with dismay.

Joshua Joseph (9)
Jubilee Primary School, Stoke Newington

My Journey From The Desert To Waterfall City

We stamp through the darkness
And tramp through the night
With horses and camels
That guide us all night.

We get off the camel
And search for the light
We sit by the beaming fire
With feet bitten by mites.

We won't give up
To get to the city
We're halfway there
But our feet don't look pretty.

We're nearly there now
We are so happy
I can see it in my mind
Please let it be true.

Kaddel Durowoju (9)
Jubilee Primary School, Stoke Newington

My Stuffed Bears

There is Mr Cool, Mr Funny
Mrs Snow and Mrs Bunny
Mr DJ, Mr Pie
Mrs Gorgeous, Mrs Shy
Mr Chicken, Mr Pen
Mrs Grumpy, Mrs Hen
But my best bear comes in handy
She looks like me and her name is Candy.

Candice Elias (10)
Jubilee Primary School, Stoke Newington

Remembering Spain

There
Where
The fruit grows on trees,
Fresh and ripe in the peaceful breeze
And taste sweet
Here,
I can't pick fruit from trees
And it's not fun.

Then,
When
The flowers were beautiful,
With pretty petals and wonderful smell
They blow in the wind.
Now,
The flowers have died
The parks look dull.

Now,
How,
In the summer holiday,
The days are bright and we can go to play,
I feel happy.
When,
I remember,
The hot sun in the fields.

Justin Cunningham (9)
Jubilee Primary School, Stoke Newington

From The Mobile Home To The Sweet Shop

We spring over fences
We fly with wings
Taking a path
That nobody knows.

We let shadows swallow us
We scramble from light
With bats and owls
Cos it gives us a fright.

We hide behind bushes
And thousands of trees
No one but me and my friends
Know which way.

We snigger at people
Ha ha, ho ho
They try to find us
But they never do.

I always wonder
If they ever will
Suddenly
We get out of the shadows of the plants and trees.

We get a glance of the gleaming sun
With cars zooming by
They come and go
In the wink of an eye.

In the quick of a flash
But slower than lightning
We see the sweet shop
We are glad and restful.

Joel Titley (8)
Jubilee Primary School, Stoke Newington

Remembering The Polish Ocean

There,
Where
In a dark blue, blue ocean,
Dolphins all around,
Salty, tasty water.
Here,
Nothing, only blank space,
Nothing but blank space.

Then,
When
Dolphins skipping in the water
I can see only reefs
In dark blue oceans.
Now,
No dolphins,
Here only fishes in the rivers.

Now,
How
Looking at the grey clouds,
Brown leaves on the grass,
Wind blowing.
Then,
I remember,
In the boat looking at the dark, dark waves.

Klaudia Barys (9)
Jubilee Primary School, Stoke Newington

My Journey From The Jungle To Paradise

In the hot jungle where wild animals live,
We drag our feet and pray we will get there,
The tigers roar and get out their claws,
The animals chase us all the way across.

In the hot, hot jungle trying to find treasure,
The animals are ready to eat just for meat,
Then the days get hotter and we are crawling to paradise,
Our bodies getting thinner as time goes on.

We try to get faster but we are flopping,
Then we all fall and try to escape from pain,
The jungle starts to howl again,
The floor is shaking and we are baking.

We are almost there,
Birds are in the air,
We can see paradise in the distance,
And the glittering sun.

Amirah Facey (9)
Jubilee Primary School, Stoke Newington

If I Had Wings

If I had wings I would see,
The moon playing hockey with the sun.

If I had wings I would hear,
People yelling down below.

If I had wings I would taste,
The burning sun, hotter than chillies.

If I had wings I could feel,
The rain scattering over my body.

Patrick Narine-Turnbull (7)
Jubilee Primary School, Stoke Newington

The Sound Collector

(Based on 'The Sound Collector' by Roger McGough)

A robber called at playtime
Wearing horrible clothes
He hid the sounds under his bed
And around the street he roved.

The shouting of the teacher
The boinging of the ball
The children who are kicking it
Up against the wall!

The strumming of guitars
The scribbling of the pencil
The children writing on paper
Ready with their stencils.

A robber called at playtime
He didn't leave a sound
He left the teachers very sad
Let's hope the sounds are found!

James Moore (8)
Jubilee Primary School, Stoke Newington

If I Had Wings

If I had wings I would smell,
The smoky sun, gassing the air.

If I had wings I would taste,
The rain as it falls.

If I had wings I would hear,
The cars driving on gravel but swooping like birds.

If I had wings I would feel,
The spikes on nests on top of trees.

Humza Sheikh (7)
Jubilee Primary School, Stoke Newington

If I Had Wings

If I had wings I would swoop
Across the stream of the blue sky.

If I had wings I could touch
The soft pillows of the clouds.

If I had wings I could see
The moon gathering her stars for bed.

If I had wings I could hear
A raindrop peep out of the clouds and say
'The coast is clear!'

Itunu Alimi (8)
Jubilee Primary School, Stoke Newington

If I Had Wings

If I had wings I would taste,
The clouds as sweet as pure sugar.

If I had wings I would smell,
The smoky burnt sun, very hot.

If I had wings I would feel,
The soft, bouncy clouds like a pillow.

If I had wings I would see,
The first drip coming out of a cloud.

Zoe Rasbash (7)
Jubilee Primary School, Stoke Newington

Ambivalent

What if I go and they don't turn up?
What if I go and they don't recognize me?
I'll see them, but will they see me?
Will they have brown eyes just like mine?
What if they have green eyes, or eyes brown like pine?
I can imagine what it will be like there when I meet them.
Those welcoming, glistening eyes like glitter sparkling.

What if I go and they come late?
What if they can't make it?
Is it such a good idea?
What if we're nothing alike?
What if I go and they're not there?
Maybe I shouldn't go.
What if I don't go?

Leigh Charles (11)
Jubilee Primary School, Stoke Newington

Heaven Is Wonderful

As I flew past the white clouds,
It felt like a dream,
Because the clouds were like pillows.
The air swirling around me tasted like the ocean,
The seagulls cried out my name, again and again,
Until I could not hear it anymore.
I then saw dolphins coming towards me,
Taking me to a bright light, high above.
I could not understand where I was,
But then I realised, I was in Heaven.

Sabina Rahman (11)
Jubilee Primary School, Stoke Newington

Chameleon

He waits, waits until,
The busy fly zooms past his nose,
Lick!
It's gone, dead, eaten
By the sly chameleon,
The deadly hunter.
He runs, runs to another branch swiftly,
It's vanished,
Gone too, like the cheeky fly.
It appears, vanishes,
Gone, gone forever.

Martha Cusker (8)
Jubilee Primary School, Stoke Newington

What Am I?

Silver coat
Flashing eyes
Savage beast
Merciless hunter
Carcass producer
Moon bayer
Silver lightning
Midnight galleon
Grey machine.

Tejas Patel (10)
Jubilee Primary School, Stoke Newington

I Have In Me

I have in me
A peaceful
Quiet
Private
Tidy bedroom

I have in me
Mellow
Empty
Sad
Calm music

I have in me
A shy
Hushed
Calm kitten

I have in me
A dry
Shady
Lovely
White clover field

I have in me a
Delicate
Shining
Bright
Glorious
Pool of sunshine

I have in me
A bowl
Of rolling
Smooth vegetables.

Nell Ranken-Perrott (8)
Jubilee Primary School, Stoke Newington

Things I'd Do If I Was Bunking . . .

Play PS2,
Computer games,
Not go to school,
Watch TV,
Watch movies,
Not go to school,
Play outside,
Go shopping,
Not go to school,
Go swimming,
Listen to CDs,
Not go to school,
Prank calls,
Plan a mutiny against the teachers,
Not go to school,
Play mobile phone games,
Basically, anything apart from work.

Francesca Titley (10)
Jubilee Primary School, Stoke Newington

My Mum

She's a comfy, cosy cushion
She's a beautiful tropical fish
She's a buzzing about bee
She's a tweeting little singing bird
She's a quiet, calm bird sleeping
She's a hot peppermint
She's the fragrance of fresh perfume
She's a steaming hot potato.

Tiffany William (9)
Jubilee Primary School, Stoke Newington

My Best Friend, Candice

My best friend is a comfy, bouncy chair
She is a snug, cuddly bed, warm and cosy
She is a kind kitten purring softly
She is a caring dolphin squeaking
She is the lively city with lights twinkling brightly
She is the quiet countryside, silent and peaceful
She is the radio playing loud music
She is the sound of children laughing
She is a hot summer afternoon with the sun setting slowly
She is an evening relaxing on the sofa drinking tea.

Leah Abraham (9)
Jubilee Primary School, Stoke Newington

Phantom Kat

My cat, Kat, is as soft and white as snow,
Her eyes are sapphires still in a waterfall,
Her nose is a ruby buried in a face of snow,
Her tongue feels like bright pink bubble bath foam,
Her ears are two pink caves beneath a carpet of snow,
Her tail is an eagle circling the sun,
Her paws are four squirrels jumping from place to place,
But she never ever walks or jumps,
Only glides forward silently through the night.

Naeema Teladia (10)
Jubilee Primary School, Stoke Newington

Witch

Potion maker
Mortal faker
Frog zapper
Wand tapper
Broomstick flyer
Cat buyer
Child snatcher
Nit catcher
High pitcher
Spot itcher
Nose picker
Human tricker
Bogey mixer.

Nazia Ahmed (10)
Jubilee Primary School, Stoke Newington

My Mum

She's a comfortable, soft sofa
She's a peaceful, sleeping cat
She's the beautiful calm sea on a warm night
She's the night sky watching over me
She's the smell of French perfume
She's a soft, peaceful piano playing
She's a daffodil that is blowing in the breeze.

Kiranjit Kaur Chohan (9)
Jubilee Primary School, Stoke Newington

Arsenal's Acrostic Poem

A lidiare is a player for Arsenal
R obert Pires too
S oon it will be a competition
E nd of training
N othing but winners
A nd one player who is our favourite
L ast but not least, Thierry Henry

F ootball is Arsenal's sport
O n the ball
O ut of the training pitch
T aking a rest at half-time
B ets are made before the match
A t full-time
L et's celebrate
L ike winners of all competitions

C old weather
L ong days
U nder control
B eating every team.

Andres Nino (9)
Jubilee Primary School, Stoke Newington

Jack The Gloomy Ghost

My name is Jack the gloomy ghost,
And I live on the Ivory Coast.
I really don't like to boast,
But I'm the scariest amongst most.

I rip your guts and eat it for dinner,
I warn you now, I really like liver.

I knock at your door at night,
I'm sure I'll give you a fright.
If you don't want a visit from me tonight,
Remember to turn off your light *not*.

Precious Couprie-Matra (10)
Jubilee Primary School, Stoke Newington

My Valentine

Roses are red, I love you
Violets for me and you
You are the red heart in my life
I will always be your wife.

Roses are red, violets are blue
Just for me and you
Will you be my valentine
Just be mine?

Kainoni Brown-Jones (9)
Jubilee Primary School, Stoke Newington

What Am I?

My first is in rap but not in fable,
My second is in acrostic and also in concrete,
My third is in kenning but not in chant,
My last is in rhyme but not in ballad,
You can write me or say me but I'm not a story.
What am I?

Liam Pegram (10)
Jubilee Primary School, Stoke Newington

The Old Judge

There was an old judge on a chair
Who thought he was losing his hair
Got jumped on by a pig
Lost his wig
And then got eaten by a bear.

Wesley Frankel (10)
Jubilee Primary School, Stoke Newington

Rain

Everybody hates rain
They think it's a real pain,
But not me
Because it comes from the sea.

I love water lots
Especially rain, it comes down in spots,
My mum thinks I'm mad
So does my dad.

Pitter, patter, I can hear
The rain knows I'm coming near,
I rush down the stairs
Past my stuffed bears.

And out I jump in the rain
I can hear it calling my name,
I am jumping up and down
I am a stupid clown.

Ruth Leah Shorten (9)
Jubilee Primary School, Stoke Newington

Dolphin Concrete Poem

I am calm and peaceful
I am sporty and alive
Gentle and kind all the time
I am silky and shiny
I'm really smooth
I shimmer through the sea
I dive like a sinking ship
We sing our peaceful tune to the moon
I see the fishes quite a lot.

Shenae Bristol (10)
Jubilee Primary School, Stoke Newington

The World

The world is not a piece of art on display,
The world is something you can't throw away.
Saturn to the Earth is so very near,
Now we should thank God that we are here.
We enjoy our days,
Where sweet God lays,
Who made the world,
God didn't make the world curled,
But made it round
And god made us hear the sound.
We listen with our ears,
Talk with our mouths
And smell with our noses.
One of the sweetest smells is the rose.
It's a wonderful world that we live in,
But some people don't use the bin.

Joseph Idris (10)
Jubilee Primary School, Stoke Newington

Who Am I?

Fast swimmer
Good diver
Water lover
Pneumonia dier
Three metre hunter
External hearer
Sensitive whiskers
Tail paddler
Trout eater
Vibration detector.

Sam Green Dorado (10)
Jubilee Primary School, Stoke Newington

The Cuidado

When I look up at the sky he's there . . .
Staring at me with those fierce, luminous blue eyes.
With functioning images, hypnotizing your . . .
Helpless,
Selfless,
Defenceless soul.
Making me feel jaded, misplaced and controlled.

The rise of the Cuidado
Strikes again!

If I dare to speak of the Devil, I'll probably die,
But all I can tell you is that I was petrified whilst I tried to hide.

The crawling that in my skin stretches beneath the dead surface,
Consuming what I feel,
Which made me confused for which was real.

Bianca Mesuria (11)
Jubilee Primary School, Stoke Newington

School

I love going to school, but the worst thing is
When my teachers roar like tigers,
The children sit like cheetahs,
The head teacher laughs like a hyena
And that's the worst thing about school!

Gabriella George (11)
Jubilee Primary School, Stoke Newington

Flowers In The Meadow

As the flowers sway in the warm wind,
Whispering among themselves like children in class,
Their colourful petals show like diamonds in the dark green grass.

The trees rock from side to side,
The wind forcing the branches to sway and move,
Their leaves usually emerald-green, silky and sometimes smooth.

With their stems, green, slender and smooth,
The strong stem standing proud and tall to keep the wondrous
flower in place,
The flowers, the trees and the grass all moving at a steady pace.

Zarah Mann (10)
Jubilee Primary School, Stoke Newington

Fireworks

My friends see fireworks
I see . . .
A bowl of salad made up of lettuce, tomatoes and yellow peppers
A backfiring bomb attacking in a combination as fast as a boxer
A witch's cauldron
Like a fountain of light that consumes our souls
A rainbow of stars lighting the sky like an enormous torch.
Wow!

Ismail Marshall (11)
Jubilee Primary School, Stoke Newington

Emerge

First there was -
A plain,
Blank,
Black,
Phlegmatic,
Big, dark area

Then . . .

The sparks flew up -
Red,
Orange,
Purple,
Blue,
Twinkling all over.
Stars sparkle -
Here,
There,
Everywhere.

Then . . .

Bang,
Bash,
Boom!

This is the evolution of our Earth.

Then we came along.
Our purpose not to wreck the Earth.
But our doings are wrecking the Earth.

Zayed Boyd (11)
Jubilee Primary School, Stoke Newington

If This Old Man

If this old man is seen by no one,
Does he exist?
If this old man is heard by no one,
Does he make a sound?
If this old man should pat my old collie,
Would he feel the shivering hand?
If this old man should drink a lemon iced tea,
Would the drink vanish down his throat?
This old man is seen by no one,
This old man is heard by no one,
This old man is me.

Samuel Collins (10)
Kerem School, Hampstead Garden Suburb

My Life

They have disappeared
They have gone forever
I have always feared this day
The big leaves droop over me
And the water weeps, drizzling down my back
My life is a disaster
I miss swinging on the stunning trees
Man is coming
I can hear him
He is stomping around destroying everything
I miss my old rainforest
I miss my life.

Jack Wagner (10)
Kerem School, Hampstead Garden Suburb

My Special Box
(Based on 'Magic Box' by Kit Wright)

I will put in my box,
The silky petals of my favourite flowers.

I will put in my box,
The leaves with that beautiful smell
From the cut down trees.

I will put in my box,
The snowflake which will never melt.

I will put in my box,
The perfume made from the crushed down roses.

I will put in my box,
Daffodils and tulips, my favourite flowers.

I will close my box
And I will keep it forever.

Yasmin Judah (9)
Kerem School, Hampstead Garden Suburb

The City

For my family
I lived in the city with a happy family
I lived in the city with my three best friends
I lived in the city with a life so great
I lived in the city with a perfect school
I lived in the city with my home so cosy and warm
But now I am far away
And the city is just a memory that fades a
                                    w
                                     a
                                      y.

Andrea Edelman (9)
Kerem School, Hampstead Garden Suburb

I Will Put In My Box

(Based on 'Magic Box' by Kit Wright)

I will put in my box . . .

The swish of a slimy snake,
The blood of a bruising buffalo,
A twig from a tiny tree.

I will put in my box . . .

A rolling ball with mud covered over it,
A drop of water trickling down,
A jumping kangaroo hopping away.

I will put in my box . . .

The sun, moon and stars
And the song of a bird singing at dawn,
And I will keep my box safely
So that it does not get lost.

Oliver Collins (9)
Kerem School, Hampstead Garden Suburb

Who?

Who is this boy I see roaming?
Swinging on the park swings,
Jumping in and out of the paddling pool,
Chewing on miniature gummy bears,
What is his name?
Where does he come from?
Why does he leave footsteps behind his trail?

Who is this boy I see from dawn to dusk?
Stacking corn cans to create a castle,
Scribbling with coloured crayons,
Resting on the school calculator,
Who is this boy?
Me?

Raymond Hanassab (10)
Kerem School, Hampstead Garden Suburb

Anger Management

When I am angry
I feel an explosion coming on.
My emotions are as turbulent
As a storm-tossed ship.

When I am angry
I feel like a kettle about to boil
And I see red.
I'm like an animal trapped in its cage.

When I am angry
I'm as agitated
As a fire-breathing dragon
Pierced through the heart with a sword.

When I am angry
I scream on my pillow
And then I realize
I am not a storm-tossed ship,
A kettle about to boil
Or a fire-breathing dragon,
But a girl who needs to take a very deep breath!

Rachel Kahn (10)
Kerem School, Hampstead Garden Suburb

Who Am I?

Who am I?
I don't know who I am.
I could be anything my mind wants me to be.
Who am I?
I could be a stranger.
Who am I?
I am a little girl playing with dolls,
Loving and caring for them as if they were real.

Kathryn Moses (11)
Kerem School, Hampstead Garden Suburb

My Magical Box

(Based on 'Magic Box' by Kit Wright)

In my magical box I will put . . .

The smile of a baby girl,
The swish of a blue wave
And the happiness of my family.

In my magical box I will put . . .

The bark of a puppy dog,
The purr of a kitten
And a whisper from my best friend.

In my magical box I will put . . .

The laughs of my brothers,
The hugs from my parents
And the gifts from my grandmas.

I will leave by my box,
The key,
And whenever I feel low,
I'll just open up my box.

Gabriella Suissa (10)
Kerem School, Hampstead Garden Suburb

On The Way To The Pink Fairy Tale Castle

'I'm bored, Daddy, how long have we been walking?'
'Look, ten minutes is not that long, so stop whining!'
'Daddy, what's in the castle?'
'A hot fudge sundae with Cinderella.'
'Daddy, hurry up, let's run!'
'Well, if I have to.'
'Daddy, it's been a really long time, when are we there?'
'Now.'

Ilana Green (10)
Kerem School, Hampstead Garden Suburb

Why Was I Mean?

Why was I mean? This is why . . .

I hit my sister
And I wouldn't eat my dinner.

Later on that day,
I didn't get my mummy
A birthday present
And my dad took me to
A Spurs game.

Later that hour,
I wouldn't walk my dog,
Neither would I tidy my room
And I was telling lies
To my parents.

That's why I was mean.

Gideon Harris (9)
Kerem School, Hampstead Garden Suburb

The Daydreamer

At first,
I thought about it hard,
Should I write about a book,
Or maybe a card?

I tried to picture things,
In my head,
I couldn't and became angry,
My face went red.

I found poems really hard,
My whole mind went blank,
Everyone had asked for more paper
And then my heart sank.

Emily Gittelmon (11)
Kerem School, Hampstead Garden Suburb

There Is In Me

There is in me a mouse.
Small. Timid. Fast.
Spends all its time running.

There is in me a kitten.
Lazy. Soft. Cute.
Looks for food to eat.

There is in me a puppy.
Playful. Alone. Hunts.
Likes to stay with its mum.

There is in me a dolphin.
Appealing. Agile. Eats fish.
Swims all day in the sea.

There is in me a leopard.
Wild. Fast. Vicious. Smart.
Hunts its prey.

There is in me a zoo
Where all my animals stay.
Some smart, some lazy
But they all like to come and play.

Liora Fox (10)
Kerem School, Hampstead Garden Suburb

My Life Is Changing

My life is changing
Metal machines have taken my home
And now the men are trying to take
My world, my friends, my family
And me!

My life is changing
Right now I'm hiding
Hiding from the humans
The humans who destroy
Destroy my world.

My life is changing
I've got nowhere else to go
The food's disappearing
The elders of the forest say
The workmen are robbers.

My life is ending
Some say they want the peacocks for their rainbow-coloured feathers
Others say they want the rhinos for their thick hide
But because I'm the last of my kind
I think, they want me!

David Gottlieb (9)
Kerem School, Hampstead Garden Suburb

My Magic Box

(Based on 'Magic Box' by Kit Wright)

I will put in my box . . .

A hat from a wizard
A white, glittering star
A laugh from a baby
A smile from a man in hospital

I will put in my box . . .

A buzzing of a bee
A croak of a cricket
A laugh from a hyena
A bark of a dog

I will put in my box . . .

The sound of a summer song
An orange autumn leaf falling from the sky
A white snowflake falling from the sky
The first blossom in spring

I shall sit on my box
Then send it to sail
On the wavy blue sea
And go where it leads me.

Joseph Greenwall-Cohen (10)
Kerem School, Hampstead Garden Suburb

An Unexpected Accident

'The ambulance isn't here, Miss.'
'It's bound to be here soon.'
'She's flooded the bathroom with tears, Miss,
What are we going to do?'

'I think she's broken her leg, Miss.'
'Don't jinx it or it will be true
And if that really does happen,
I'll blame it all on you.'

'Her mum is on her way now, Miss,
We've got nothing to worry about.'
'If you say that again, dear,
I'm really going to shout.'

'Her mum is in the building, Miss,
But she's about to die from shock.'
'Comfort her, comfort her,
Before her heart stops.'

'I'm really, really sorry, Miss,
But the poem's got to go,
I hope her leg is OK now,
But I guess we'll never know.'

Sabrina Zeloof (9)
Kerem School, Hampstead Garden Suburb

My Sister

My sly little sister
So naughty but kind,
She is so mischievous,
However, I don't mind.

Her devilish laugh,
Makes me oh, so glad,
But when she starts crying,
She starts going mad.

When I'm feeling down,
She tries to help me out,
But when she's in a mood,
She starts to scream and shout.

She is ever so cute,
I want to pinch her cheeks,
If I was doing that,
It would take me weeks and weeks.

Her hits are rather hard,
Her scratches are quite tough,
If she was a famous wrestler,
I think she'd be the most rough.

However, she is my sister,
A very kind girl,
I love her so much,
She's as pure as a pearl.

Solomon Ishack (11)
Kerem School, Hampstead Garden Suburb

I Will Put In My Box . . .

(Based on 'Magic Box' by Kit Wright)

I will put in my box
A bag of pink petals

I will put in my box
A container of camp memories

I will put in my box
The love for my family

I will put in my box
A sack of my memories of Switzerland

I will put in my box
My jewellery from different countries

I will put in my box
My stamp collection

I will put my box
On a ship and watch it sail into the ocean.

Yael Yamin-Joseph (10)
Kerem School, Hampstead Garden Suburb

A Little Bumblebee!

One summer's day,
A red rose had grown,
I flew straight to it,
Right from my home.

A handful of pollen,
A breath of fresh air,
Mix them together
And my honey is there.

I gathered it,
Every bit,
And took it to my hive.
When I had finished it,
There was nothing left inside!

Lillie Miller (11)
Kerem School, Hampstead Garden Suburb

The Time Machine

If there was such a thing
As a time machine
That could stop war
What would the world be like?

A big, metal machine
I would like to make
Maybe I could change history
What would the world be like?

If the Arabs didn't fight the Jews
And there was no war
If Hitler had not been born
What would the world be like?

Maybe my friends will help me
As well as the rest of the world
Maybe I could change events and dates
What would the world be like?

My decision is made
I am going to build it
And then maybe I will know
What the world would be like.

Laura Baker (11)
Kerem School, Hampstead Garden Suburb

The Stranger Within Me

Besides the countless red roses,
I notice as I walk by,
Besides the endless path,
I notice as I walk by,
Besides a strange girl,
I notice I don't know.
Who is she?

Why is it
She follows my footsteps in the day
And the minute I touch water,
Her sweet, passionate body dissolves
In me?

Besides a strange girl,
I notice she follows me,
Besides her footsteps,
I notice they follow me.

I look at her,
I see her on the swings,
Alone,
Bullied,
I look at her again,
But there she is,
Not a single inch away,
I look around,
No swings.

Besides the multicoloured flowers,
I notice as I walk by,
Besides a strange girl,
I notice I don't know,
Besides my childhood,
I notice,
My reflection . . .
Me.

Ariella Aghai (10)
Kerem School, Hampstead Garden Suburb

I Will Put In My Picture . . .

(Based on 'Magic Box' by Kit Wright)

I will put in my picture . . .

A squashed snowman with a big smile,
A funny fish from the ocean,
A lovely lady with long, gold hair
And a small, silver seal.

I will put in my picture . . .

A witch with a cat on a broomstick,
A little girl playing in the snow,
An old man with an old book
And a dog playing with a cat.

I will put in my picture . . .

A cafeteria in a clever town,
A sweet star in the sky,
The sun sending happiness
And the moon singing in the night.

So I know what to draw,
And I know what to do,
I just have one problem,
I don't know where the paper and the colours are!

Naomi Revel (9)
Kerem School, Hampstead Garden Suburb

The Seasons Of The Year

The summer bird sings a graceful song,
The breeze is so warm,
I love the birds humming along.

The autumn is a thrill,
Especially when the leaves fall under the trees,
I play for a long, long time outside.

The winter wind is chilling,
Lots of snow is fun to throw,
Your mum tells you to come inside for a hot bath.

Now the spring term is here,
Buttercups and daffodils smelling lovely,
The whole year is fun.

Arthur Caplin (10)
Kerem School, Hampstead Garden Suburb

My Magic Box

(Based on 'Magic Box' by Kit Wright)

I will put in the box . . .
The sound of a whale as it floats on the sea crying for salvation
I would take a baby cub as it is a ravishingly beautiful animal.

I will put in my box . . .
My mum as I will treasure her forever
A first smile of a cuddly monkey and
My best friend, Jamal.

My box is fashioned
From gold steel and love, and on the lid
There is a picture of my mum
And on the sides my best friend, Jamal.

Leanne Webb-Mills (11)
Nightingale Primary School, Wood Green

The Test

The sun is blazing through the window.
I hear a song whistling constantly through the air.
My heart pounds through the warm breeze of summer.
The sea running a marathon, beating the tides to the shore.
I rapidly run my long nails through my hair.
It waves fiercely at my rough handling.
I gaze through the window, constantly wondering when it will end.
I clench my fist, tempted to get up and run far away through the
                                        depths of the corridor.
I hear that sound, that familiar sound, that deflates my heart in relief.
It is over.
The test is over.

Jackie Moore (11)
Nightingale Primary School, Wood Green

Sounds

I love the sound of music.
I hate the sound of doors crashing.
I love the sound of children screaming.
I hate the sound of the tap dripping.
I love the sound of thunder crashing.
I hate the sound of my mum shouting.
I love the sound of people stamping.
I hate the sound of cats purring.
I love the sound of dogs barking.
I hate the sound of clocks ticking.
I love the sound of someone kicking the ball.
I hate the sound of people eating.

Sean Gallagher (8)
Nightingale Primary School, Wood Green

Feeling Lonely

When you feel lonely
It's like a bird caged up
With no one to cheer him up.

It's like no one wants to play with you
Or you don't get picked to play a game.
When you feel lonely,
You just want to be with somebody, doing something.

But no, you're all alone in your bedroom,
Trying to liven yourself up and playing with teddy,
Combing your Barbie doll's hair, thinking to yourself,
What should I do? Who wants to play with me?

Don't you feel lonely when you get left out
And everything's on your back?
You just want to break free,
Start over a new life, at least playing with someone, somewhere.

Geniene Miller (10)
Nightingale Primary School, Wood Green

Sounds

I love the sound of Sean Paul rapping.
I hate the sound of people banging.
I love the sound of shoes tapping.
I hate the sound of my brother snoring.
I love the sound of people speaking.
I hate the sound of people stamping.
I love the sound of dogs barking.

Shanice Clarke (7)
Nightingale Primary School, Wood Green

The Boy Who Learnt To Kill

One night I heard my mum crying, crying as she lay,
Why isn't she praying? That's all my mind could say.
I came to give her a cuddle and she said,
'Your father was rushed to hospital while you were in bed.'

Something in my heart made me say,
'I must find that person who took my father away.'
From that day forward I looked for people who did crimes,
Me myself have been in fights all at different times.

When I thought I found that person, I punched him to the ground,
Trying to make him admit that he brought my father down.
Right there and then I watched his eyes close,
Dead on the floor, no air from his nose.

Now I realized what I'd done,
I am a criminal, I killed someone.
That night in bed I heard my mum speaking to the police about what she'd done,
She was the one who killed my father.

Shamika Davis (9)
Nightingale Primary School, Wood Green

Moonlight

When the moon rises, the night sky shines
The cats come out and miaow at the sky
A big storm scares the cats and birds
The cats scratch at the roof.

The birds fly high to their nests
And the cats hide in their houses
The sound of the storm scares the animals
In the rainforest.

At the end of the storm
All the animals come out
And look at the sunny sky.

Taylor Stoakes (9)
Nightingale Primary School, Wood Green

My Magic Box

(Based on 'Magic Box' by Kit Wright)

I will put in the box . . .

The sound of the dolphins jumping in and out of the sea,
The coconut of a precious palm tree,
The purr of a newborn kitten.

I will put in the box . . .

The smell of Carribean food,
A woman wearing a golden chain
And a feather from a golden eagle.

I will put in the box . . .

The sun shining brightly under sea,
A cowboy in a space shuttle
And an astronaut on a white pony.

My box is fashioned with white, golden silk,
Gold, silver and bronze
And the sun on both sides
With hearts on the corners.

I shall ride in my box
Across the seven seas
Into the blue tropical beach
And sit and watch the exotic sea.

Allisia Ngbanzo (11)
Nightingale Primary School, Wood Green

Colours

I love the colour of school,
I hate the colour of sun,
I love the colour of a rainbow,
I hate the colour of paper,
I love the colour of birds,
I hate the colour of cats.

Stavros Zangoulos (7)
Nightingale Primary School, Wood Green

Snowfall

Peaceful village
Mountain edge
Snowy peaks
Sliding sledge
Whooshing rush
White cloud
Covering sky
Crashing loud
Booming thunder
Rocks tumble
Skiers shouting
Climbers stumble
Rush of wind
Stormy force
Battering ram
With no remorse
Piling snow
Plummeting through
Sheet of white
Dash of blue
Hidden village
Tree and branch
Giant blankness
Avalanche!

Jack Twomey (9)
Nightingale Primary School, Wood Green

Monkeys

M onkeys, monkeys, everywhere,
O n the jungle trees with no underwear!
N o one sees their mischievous grins,
K angaroos think monkeys have fins!
E verywhere and anywhere they'll always be cheeky,
Y ou'll find that they're acting freaky!
S winging from tree to tree. That's not fair!

Shani Thompson-Ellis (10)
Nightingale Primary School, Wood Green

Alone

I live under a lamp post.
As the day goes past,
I watch the city
    And wait
Until the lights go off
    At last,
So I can rest
    In peace,
Without the least sound
    At all.

The wind is rattling,
The wind is blowing
And once again it's snowing.
My feet are swollen
And my nose is blocked.
I hear a shout,
That brings a doubt,
That I shouldn't be living here
    Anymore.

Omar Ibrahim (10)
Nightingale Primary School, Wood Green

Far Away

Think of me when you're happy,
Think of me when you're sad,
Think of me when you're lonely,
I'll always be your friend.

Aimee Barratt (8)
Nightingale Primary School, Wood Green

Summer

S tart the day with no school,
U nderwater is much more cool,
M ates are here so it's party time,
M yths and legends left all behind,
E scape from school and into the sun
R ush outside and have some fun.

H appy children playing everywhere,
O utings are great, just like the States,
L ace up tight for a race,
I ce creams are for tasty treats,
D onkey rides on the beach,
A pples, apricots, glisten to my eyes,
Y ummy yum yum, it's ice cream,
S ummertime is just for me!

Mithunaa Upendra (10)
Nightingale Primary School, Wood Green

Moaning Mountain

I'm
All on my
Own, if you
Listen hard you'll
Hear my groan. I'll
Moan and groan all
Day long, sometimes it
Might even seem like a song.
If you try to climb me, you won't
Succeed because I am the friend you
Do not need! My jagged sides will rip you
Apart, until my sharp sides have got to your heart.
For my inside is ice-cold, there, now you've been told what
I'll do to you if you try to climb me, for I am the *moaning mountain!*

Hannah Langley (10)
Nightingale Primary School, Wood Green

The Punk

Spikes,
Sneers,
No cheer.

All you see are wild, bright colours,
Studs,
Rings and chokers.

Piercings,
Tattoos,
Different point of view.

That's the punk,
Don't care what people think,
They stand out,
They're special.

Talah-Kati Kaddourah (10)
Nightingale Primary School, Wood Green

My Brother

He stinks
He's rude
He always calls me names
He's dumb
But sometimes he's calm.

Hannah Zawedde (8)
Nightingale Primary School, Wood Green

Weather

Thunder dashed violently through the clouds.
Lightning crashed the windows with a shock.
Storm tumbled as the glass was broken.
Fog began to spread out some dirty dust.
Rain splattered water over the mountains.
Ice froze as the world was covered.
Wind blew over houses with a surprise.
Frost began to snow over people's roads.
Sunshine fell with a hot place that was drowned.
Snow began to fall with cold weather.

Wind is a bad weather with a whirlpool.
Tornado is a violent weather with a shock.
Weathers can be bad as it could but floods
Floods can drown people by their breathing
Breathing is very important for weather
Rain can make a flood by the thunder
Thunder is as a bad weather for people
Snow is not the strongest weather ever.

Nageswari Samy (9)
Nightingale Primary School, Wood Green

The Man From China

There was once a man from China,
He was a very good miner.
He dug underground,
But couldn't turn round,
So he swung his pick with all his might
And began to see a bit of light.
When he got out, he began to shout,
'Where am I?'
The next day he entered a race,
But the other people were too fast.
He came last!

Archie Parker (8)
Norfolk House School, Muswell Hill

The Sun

The sun is like a big bun
It is boiling hot.
Everyone says it is fun
And I like it a lot.

It lightens up the day
And helps the flowers grow.
We can go out to play
But Dad has grass to mow.

It is best to stay inside
When it is really hot!
Wear a hat outside
Or you will burn a lot!

Levent Latif-Maeer (8)
Norfolk House School, Muswell Hill

I Like Football

I like football,
The things I like are
Rolling in mud,
Slide tackling,
Jumping,
Building walls.
I don't like getting hit,
I don't like other teams.
But I like being deadly.

Nathan Grieve (9)
Norfolk House School, Muswell Hill

Pets!

Small pets are cute,
Dogs chew your boot.
Cat pets are hard to beat,
Hamsters are very sweet.
Parrot pets can copy you,
Guinea pigs can tickle you.
Fish pets are waterbound,
Insects creep and crawl around.
Rabbit pets keep twitching,
Horses need grooming.
Samoyed pets are madly hairy,
Spiders can be rather scary.
Dolphins are too big to keep
And they're not really very cheap.
If you look hard enough it's true,
You'll find a pet that's right for you!

Freya Godfrey (11)
Norfolk House School, Muswell Hill

Simba And Jinx

We've just got two new kittens
And I am absolutely smitten!

One is a tabby and is called Simba,
Sometimes known as Mr Wimber!
The other is black and is called Jinx,
And this one is such a minx!

They lie on their backs
When they're relaxed,
They play with the carpet on the stairs,
Dad hopes it won't need any repairs!

I love them both with all my heart,
And could never imagine being apart.

Christie Malva (11)
Norfolk House School, Muswell Hill

My Hamster, Emily

My hamster's name is Emily,
She really is quite fat,
Because she eats so heavily
And it seems that that is that!

She has a short and stubby tail,
With soft and fluffy fur,
And often tries to chew our mail,
But oh, I still love her!

She has a personality,
Which also can be rare,
She'll sit up and look at me,
Like a round, sweet, little bear.

And yes, my hamster, Emily,
Will groom herself, then crouches,
And while I watch her merrily,
She starts filling up her pouches.

Valentina Wright (10)
Norfolk House School, Muswell Hill

Not Even The Moon

Nothing is as beautiful as you,
Yes, the moon may sparkle and shimmer,
Glimmer in the still night air,
But in the morning does she stay?
No, she simply fades away.

Lily Callanan (9)
Norfolk House School, Muswell Hill

I Had A Dream Last Night

I had a dream last night,
But I can't quite remember what it was about.
At the time it gave me a fright,
But luckily I didn't shout!

I had a dream last night,
Although it's very dim,
It was someone playing with a kite,
My best friend Tim.

I had a dream last night,
One bit was very scary,
When the monster saw me he took a bite,
That's when I realised he was very hairy!

I had a dream last night,
It was a big fright,
Now I've told you my dream,
You can tell me yours.

Adam Nickless-Wright (9)
Norfolk House School, Muswell Hill

Fighting Clock

Hickory, dickory, dock,
Two mice ran up the clock.
The clock struck one,
But that was only the young son.
The father thought he should run
In case it struck two.

Dónal Breen Carroll (11)
Our Lady and St Joseph Primary School, Hackney

Sounds In The Mornings

The city:
In the city, cars drive past,
Making noises that don't last,
People are travelling to their work,
Noises are being made by some jerks.

Big Ben makes its sounds,
While lots of visitors are around,
Men are fixing roads,
Bang, bang, they go.

The airport:
In the mornings, miaow go the aeroplanes,
In the station, choo choo go the trains,
Chat, chat, chat go the people,
People staring at the treacle.

The village:
Cock-a-doodle-doo, can you hear the chicken?
Bang, bang, go the adults licking,
Sweep, sweep go the children sweeping,
While others are sleeping.

Delawoe Adjaklo (11)
Our Lady and St Joseph Primary School, Hackney

Wishes

I wish I could fly
Up high in the sky
I wish I could stay
With you and your way
I wish I could see
What you mean for me
And God will watch over us
Forever and ever
          Amen.

Jasmin Alvarez (11)
Our Lady and St Joseph Primary School, Hackney

There Once Was A Time

There once was a time
In the middle of September
And something happened
That I'll always remember.

I got to school at half-past eight
And it started to rain
And as I got into my class
I saw my teacher with a cane.

She said, 'Young man, why are you late?'
I said, 'It's only half-past eight.'
She said, 'I don't care what you say,
You're due to get smacked anyway!'

I went back home in a great big moan
And a car was passing by
I ran right into the open street
For I just wanted to die.

Michael Iheanyichukwu Nnanna-Dikeocha (11)
Our Lady and St Joseph Primary School, Hackney

Love

This morning when I wakened
And saw the sun above
I softly said, 'Good morning, Lord,
Bless everyone I love.'
And right away I thought of you
And said a loving prayer,
That He would bless you especially
And keep you free from care.
I thought of all the happiness
A day can hold in store,
I wished it all for you because
No one deserves it more.

Jodie Smith (10)
Our Lady and St Joseph Primary School, Hackney

What A Ring

Once upon a time
On a dirty line
I saw something that was fine
I wanted it to be mine.

That thing on the dirty line
Was not mine
So I made it fine
And claimed it as mine.

Someone saw me with the thing
It was a golden diamond ring
They started to sing
About this very great ring.

The thing about this ring
Was it was such a shiny thing
I was lucky to have it on me
I had to go home for tea.

When I got home
My mum was on the phone
Saying they had lost something
Oh, it was my golden diamond ring.

Janet Esan (11)
Our Lady and St Joseph Primary School, Hackney

Valentine Rose

You've filled my heart for quite a while,
You sail through my mind like the River Nile.
My heart was broke but now repaired,
When I'm with you I don't feel scared.
I've tried talking or sending a sign,
But now I'll say it . . .
'Will you be my valentine?'

Johnnie O'Brien (10)
Our Lady and St Joseph Primary School, Hackney

The Wicked Wizard And Valentine Fairy Poem

The wicked wizard lived in a black palace on the mountains.
He was young, mean and tall,
Ugly as a street cat, tough as a black bat.
He made me feel irritated like I had ants in my pants.
The wicked wizard reminded me of the witches and wizards stories.

The valentine fairy lived in a grand palace.
She was old, beautiful and loving,
Kind as a friend, never tried to pretend.
She made me feel like the whole world cared about me.
The valentine fairy reminded me of Saint Valentine.

Susanna Fasasi (10)
Our Lady and St Joseph Primary School, Hackney

The Smelly King Kong

The smelly King Kong
Is a legendary king
A mean lean machine
As hard as steel
As thick as rocks
It makes me feel like dirt
It makes me want to take a bath
The smelly King Kong
It makes me want to hurl.

Jack O'Kane (11)
Our Lady and St Joseph Primary School, Hackney

Excuses

Head: 'Late again, Richard. What's the excuse this time?'
Child: 'Not my fault, sir.'
Head: 'Whose is it then?'
Child: 'The bus driver, sir.'
Head: 'What did he do?'
Child: 'Went the wrong say, miss.'
Head: 'What did you call me?'
Child: 'Umm, I called you 'sir', yeah I called you 'sir'.'
Head: 'Anyway, I heard that excuse five times this week. I went on
           the bus and it was fine.'
Child: 'But he's mad.'
Head: 'Now where's your lines from yesterday?'
Child: 'Bus driver has them.'
Head: 'What? Why does he have them?'
Child: 'Like I told you, sir. Mad, sir.'

Olushola Awoyejo (11)
Our Lady and St Joseph Primary School, Hackney

Mean But Funny!

Snake's on a road
Like a big, fat toad
That's what I wish for you

A pain in the log
Wanna see my dog
Please, please don't come near my frog

Keep out of sight
Because you just might
Start a fight with my knight

Don't show your face
Around this place
It will crack on my small case.

Shevon Corbett (10)
Our Lady and St Joseph Primary School, Hackney

All About My Sister

She always gets on my nerves,
She never ever shuts up.
She is always getting up my nose.

She is always watching TV, never stops,
She sleeps for long and never wakes up.
She is always talking on the phone,
She was once on it for two hours.
She is always getting up my nose.

Sometimes she is my friend
And sometimes she is not,
She can always be a pain in the butt.
She really gets up my nose.

Sometimes she can be an angel,
But sometimes not.
She really gets on my nerves.
She really gets up my nose.

Sandra Queiros (11)
Our Lady and St Joseph Primary School, Hackney

The Cutey

The adorable princess
Slept in her bed
Dreaming, sleeping and resting
As beautiful as a rose
Just smell her toes
I think she's a beauty
Just like a cutey
The adorable princess
Reminds me she's going
To be a queen.

Betty Hotesso (10)
Our Lady and St Joseph Primary School, Hackney

Silly Rhyme

Once upon a time
I had a silly rhyme
It was all about a crime
It was sour like lemon and lime.

It was in a nasty place
Where a witch lived, never to show her face
Where her life was a horrible case
Her surroundings were nothing but waste.

There was a boy named Jim
Had a friend called Tim
He lived to win
Always loved to play with pins.

He had a horror dare
Which was to go and scare
The witch in her ditch
Sorry, but that's where it ends.

See why I said it was a silly rhyme
Because there is no crime!

Jennifer Esan (11)
Our Lady and St Joseph Primary School, Hackney

Would You Be My Valentine

I have never been touched like this in my heart before,
I want to love you more and more.
Would you please be my valentine?
'Cause I only want you to be mine.
When I think of you I get a tingle in my spine.

When I saw you first, it was love at first sight,
You are just like my sun, you shine so bright.
Would you please be my valentine?
'Cause I only want you to be mine.

Martin Mazina (11)
Our Lady and St Joseph Primary School, Hackney

I Don't Like That

I don't want
Nothing to eat for a morning feast
(It gave people the impression I was a food beast).

I don't want
To jump
(Because I'll need my asthma pump).

I don't want
Meat to eat
(Because I'm a vegetarian and don't let me repeat)!

I don't want
Nothing to eat for lunch
(I've already had a monster sized munch).

I don't need
No goodnight prayer
(Because frankly I don't even care).

I don't want
Nothing to eat for dinner
(It makes me sound like no winner).

I don't want
A midnight feast
(Give me some space, or room at least).

I don't want
A ball to catch
(You and me will never match).

Last but not least I have to say:
I would not like them here or there
I would not like them anywhere
I do not like what you're giving me
I do not like them, so just let me be!

Aisha Hill (11)
Our Lady and St Joseph Primary School, Hackney

It's All Big!

In a very big town
There was a very big king
And this very big king
Had a very big ring.

And this very big king
Had a very big house
And in this very big house
Had a very big sink.

This very big sink
Wasn't for a drink
It was to wash his
Big, fat diamond ring.

The ring was big
The ring was shiny
It was shinier than a shining shimmy!

Nwamuka Uzomba (11)
Our Lady and St Joseph Primary School, Hackney

My Local Area

My local area is flashing
But people think it's smashing
People think there's millions of flats and houses
But there is really billions
People think it's busy
And it's rather noisy
People keep on bashing
Then me and my mum keep mashing.

Brógan Slade (8)
St John The Evangelist RC Primary School, Islington

This Is My Area

I think Islington is flashing,
But people think it's smashing.

My area is haunted,
But I think it's heated.

Islington has lots of toys,
But it's full of boys,
This is my area.

In the morning it's peaceful,
But in the afternoon it's pouring.

Children keep on teaming,
But I think they're screaming.

Islington is a place for running,
But it is also cunning,
This is my area.

Helen Teklehaimont (8)
St John The Evangelist RC Primary School, Islington

Dizzy Gazing

Flashing
Squashing
Road-like snake
Windy cars
Zoom they make
My sister screams
Dashing
Bashing.

Andrew Hunter-Pires (8)
St John The Evangelist RC Primary School, Islington

Down By The River

Down by the river,
Mark met a rabbit,
It was hopping around,
Looking for a carrot.

Down by the river,
Mark met a squirrel,
Running around,
Looking for some nuts.

Down by the river,
Mark met a beaver,
Creeping around,
Looking for a slippery fish.

Down by the river,
Mark met a mouse,
Scuttling around,
Looking for a house.

Brogan Hutton (7)
St John The Evangelist RC Primary School, Islington

What I Think Of School

I don't like school,
It's not very cool,
I would rather jump in a swimming pool,
The work is boring,
I'd rather start snoring,
Teachers, teachers, give us the creeps,
I think we are learning not to think,
The toilets stink of rotten ink.

Oisín Teevan (9)
St John The Evangelist RC Primary School, Islington

My Beautiful Pony

My beautiful pony
Gallops fast and freely
Before she nibbles grass
She takes rich people on her back
Up the hill

Her baby pony has a long pink tail
Adorable baby-blue eyes
And a pleasant brownish colour skin

You will find my beautiful pony
On a farm
In a zoo
And even in the jungle

When my beautiful pony is happy
She pounces on her hay
And makes a neigh neigh neighing sound.

Angela Parisi (8)
St John The Evangelist RC Primary School, Islington

The Dragon Of Fire

The dragon of fire is a fierce dragon,
One look of its eyes, you'll be in fear,
Until the night dies,
He can destroy two castles,
With one blow of fire.
He can make you out of a tyre,
The people fight, with all their might,
They get hurt once or twice,
Then they say, I'm not going to be nice!
The dragon dies and looks at the people's eyes!

Diogo Ferreira (9)
St John The Evangelist RC Primary School, Islington

My Horse

My pretty horse races fast
On its four strong legs
When she's happy she wags her straight brown bushy tail
Her skin is nice and smooth and furry
She likes people stroking and brushing her fur
She does what I say
She stands up, waits then sprints and gallops off
We often find her in a farm or in the big zoo
She has beautiful bright eyes
Her mane has bits of yellow highlights
My pretty horse is colourful and beautiful
She makes lots of neighing sounds
But always wears a smile on her pretty face.

Fiona Corcoran (9)
St John The Evangelist RC Primary School, Islington

The Cat

The cat's name is Diamond,
She searches for her prey,
She quietly does a cat walk,
Then she pounces,
She bounces,
She throws her lunch away,
Because she wants to eat mice instead, today,
She plays before she attacks her prey,
The little mouse is grey and white,
It nibbles cheese all day and night!

Marrione Ronlyn Worrel (9)
St John The Evangelist RC Primary School, Islington

The Robin

The lovely robin chirps when she sings
Before she eats some slobbering, slimy worms
She hovers slowly
With her lovely hazel wings
Glittering in the sun

As she lands on the ground
She slowly jumps up and own
She walks carefully
Looking left and right
When she sees a cunning fox
She hovers safely into a tree
Where her nest is.

Monique Moloney (9)
St John The Evangelist RC Primary School, Islington

Upper Street

Red is the colour of hair
Also, I get so sweaty
I get as red as a bus

Blue is a Ferrari
Drove past Upper Street
It is as fast as a cheetah
Which is fast

Green is the colour of a tree
Hot in Upper Street
Only in the summer.

Thomas Carlin (8)
St John The Evangelist RC Primary School, Islington

Where I Live

Islington is where I live,
The road is like a snake.

The cars on the road are like a stampede of bulls,
I would love to make the cars stop by a few chains and pulls.

In the morning on Sunday it is great,
But in the afternoon, I hate.

It's outrageous - the noise!

Islington is full of mice,
Everyone says it's cold as ice.

I go away, out to play,
That's Islington.

Lauren Speirs (8)
St John The Evangelist RC Primary School, Islington

Tips For Islington

I like my local area,
S o use your ears and listen,
L ook at the lamppost glisten,
I slington is so crowded and busy,
N ever walk around because you will get dizzy,
G o and let the children play,
T here's a football match today,
O h you must see Upper Street, it's the busiest place,
N ever look at a stranger directly in the face.

Johnny Costa (8)
St John The Evangelist RC Primary School, Islington

Seasons In Islington

In the autumn
In Islington,
When leaves fall,
They fall like pieces of paper.

In the winter
In Islington,
When the rain falls,
It falls like people's tears.

In the spring
In Islington,
When flowers bloom,
They bloom like children.

In the summer
In Islington,
When leaves turn green,
They turn as green as . . .
Frogs!

Saoirse Ní Cheallaigh (8)
St John The Evangelist RC Primary School, Islington

Noisy Lift

I was walking in the park,
Suddenly I saw a car crash,
It made a very loud *smash!*
It was busy by the car,
My area is crazy,
Traffic is like a herd of elephants,
I tell the police but I need evidence,
Somebody help, help.

Sam Gorrand (8)
St John The Evangelist RC Primary School, Islington

Down By The Jungle

Down by the jungle,
Adam met a rat,
It was running in circles,
Looking for a safe place to hide.

Down by the jungle,
Victor met a lion,
It was sneaking around,
Looking for its prey.

Down by the jungle,
Abel met a monkey,
Swinging on some branches,
Looking for bananas to eat.

Down by the jungle,
Alfie met a snake,
Slithering on the grass,
Hiding from a tiger.

Anthony Ngo (7)
St John The Evangelist RC Primary School, Islington

On My Street

On my street the pavement is quiet,
But the road is a riot.
Down the road is the Mall,
With its great white walls.
On Upper Street there's so many shops,
Surprisingly there are no cops.
And, finally, the school fleet,
Who come from Duncan Street.
London is a busy place,
Everybody acts like they're in a race.

Conor Flannery-Mann (8)
St John The Evangelist RC Primary School, Islington

As . . .

As big as a whale,
As small as a spider,
As long as a snake,
As fast as a cheetah,
As fierce as a lino,
As strong as a gorilla,
As slow as a tortoise,
As fat as an elephant,
As wet as a shark,
As poisonous as a wasp,
As . . .

Yonata Addis (7)
St John The Evangelist RC Primary School, Islington

Islington

I like my local area,
S o listen to me now,
L ike a kitten purring,
I will show you what Islington is all about,
N ow, people throw things on the floor,
G lance through people's doors,
T o know about my local town,
O h, come and have a visit,
N o, don't smash the house!

Tobi Akinboboye (8)
St John The Evangelist RC Primary School, Islington

As . . .

As big as a gorilla,
As tiny as an ant,
As fast as a lion,
As grumpy as a bear,
As small as a rat,
As fat as an elephant,
As tall as a giraffe,
As huge as a whale,
As jumpy as a monkey,
As long as a snake.

Marie Kohlert (7)
St John The Evangelist RC Primary School, Islington

My Scarecrow

Straw for his head,
Stones for his eyes,
Carrot for his nose,
String for his mouth,
Sticks for his hands,
Shaggy coat,
Two sticks for his legs.

Ben Righaleto (7)
St John The Evangelist RC Primary School, Islington

As . . .

As big as an elephant,
As fast as a rabbit,
As fierce as a dinosaur,
As scary as a ghost,
As strong as a rhinoceros,
As small as a mouse,
As touch as a rat,
As big as a house,
As smooth as a tiger,
As fat as a pig,
As hairy as a bear.

Abel Testay (7)
St John The Evangelist RC Primary School, Islington

Maybe

Maybe you can come to my house,
Maybe you can stay,
Maybe we can go to the funfair,
Maybe we can stay up late,
Maybe we can draw pictures,
Maybe we can paint,
Maybe we can go swimming,
Maybe we can go to the lake.

Courtney Mullen (7)
St John The Evangelist RC Primary School, Islington

As . . .

As wild as a leopard,
As small as a mouse,
As hungry as a tiger,
As tall as a giraffe,
As strong as a bull,
As tiny as an ant,
As fierce as a lion,
As slippery as a fish,
As big as an ostrich.

Sarah Cluskey (7)
St John The Evangelist RC Primary School, Islington

Tall As A Tower

Tall as a tower,
Longer than a train,
Spookier than a ghost,
Funnier than a joker,
Stronger than a rhino,
Smaller than an ant,
Faster than a cheetah,
Knows more than a wizard.

Ciaran Daniels (7)
St John The Evangelist RC Primary School, Islington

Down By The Dump

Down by the dump
I met a rat,
It was running around
Escaping from the cat.

Down by the dump
I met a snail,
Leaving a long slimy trail.

Down by the dump
I met a cat,
He was sneaking around
Looking for the rat.

Adam Connolly (7)
St John The Evangelist RC Primary School, Islington

Life In Upper Street

On Upper Street it is very narrow,
Some people carry a wheelbarrow,
Lights on Upper Street are always flashing
And I really think they are smashing.
Some people are always pushing
And carrying a cushion,
Upper Street is my favourite street,
All the people use their feet.

Louis Comerford (8)
St John The Evangelist RC Primary School, Islington

My Little Sister

My sister is really bad
She's two-faced too
When I'm told to get her a drink
She'll come with me
I think to myself *why is she following me?*
With her nasty grin
Um, maybe she's planning one of her evil plans
As soon as I give her the drink
She giggles and drops it
My mum comes rushing down the stairs
My mum sighs
'Who did this?'
Then my little sister puts on her innocent look
And then talks sweetly
'It was Kezia!'
As soon as I reach out to strangle her
My mum starts yelling at me
So I run to my room and start planning my revenge
I took out her homework and started scribbling
She went berserk and she got in trouble.

Kezia Dwomoh
St Monica's RC Primary School, Hackney

Da Boy

In da world
In da country
In da city
In da house
There is . . . da boy
Called Dara.

Christian Kyei (11)
St Monica's RC Primary School, Hackney

Forever Friends

F un to be with.
O nly option is to be with you.
R espectful to everyone.
E specially you.
V ery sweet to you.
E nthusiastic when with you.
R eassuring when you're uncertain.

F orgiving at all times.
R esponsible at all times.
I nteresting whatever the matter.
E ntertains you all the time.
N eeds you the same way you need them.
D earest to your heart.
S ecrets are shared between you and them.

Laura Idowu
St Monica's RC Primary School, Hackney

Friends

F orever kind and understanding
R eady to stand by your side whatever the circumstances
I nside your heart there is a unique place
E ver ready to make you smile
N ever hurtful but always helpful
D ay by day your love grows stronger
S ent by God from Heaven, especially for you.

Okuns Aibangbee (11)
St Monica's RC Primary School, Hackney

Tick-Tock Clock

Tick-tock clock don't stop
Two people like a flower
On a rock

Tick-tock clock don't stop
I see one woman
With a mop

Tick-tock clock don't stop
I don't see the dock
Near the lock

Tick-tock clock don't stop
I hear a man's name
Called Alsop

Tick-tock clock
It's gonna stop.

Meshach Philip (9)
St Monica's RC Primary School, Hackney

School

School is great, school is cool
It is the greatest thing that can happen to you
You can learn a lot of things
If you can pay attention
If you don't, you can end up in detention
If you learn stuff a lot of times
You may get a surprise
With chocolate and sweets
Remember, school is great!

Darren Kissi
St Monica's RC Primary School, Hackney

Come Together

Come together all ye people so we can share some love,
It's not about reputations but coming together as a nation,
We can shout or scream but later on
We'll see that we must come together

Everybody can find their peace in themselves if they try
But we have to teach ourselves how to abide
But there is one way of doing this
So let us come together as one

Friends and family are always there for you
But I am sure there are other people who care for you too
If you really want to know let us all come together

So if you're reading this poem
And don't believe it's good
Well you better think again
Because this is coming from the hood
But I know violence is not the answer
So let us come together.

Samuel Folayan (11)
St Monica's RC Primary School, Hackney

Stranger Passing By

I've waited for you when the wind blew hard,
When the world was to turned upside-down,
But a stranger like you has left me drowning in the sea,
A stranger like you has mocked me,
When my friends were against me you joined them and laughed,
So stranger, why have you come back to me?
Tell me, stranger
Are you here to laugh, to mock me once more?
Are you to tear every path I walk
Or have you changed and come to join me?
A stranger like you can be called a butterfly passing by and by,
Oh stranger, I'm glad that you're passing once more,
Oh stranger, I'm glad you've come to join me.

Victoria Bangu-Pichel (11)
St Monica's RC Primary School, Hackney

Lovely

Let is join hands,
Let us celebrate,
We are one nation,
It doesn't matter if
You are white or black.

Let us just celebrate,
Let us come together
As a whole nation,
Put a smile on your face,
It is a lovely world, hurrah!

It doesn't matter, let's celebrate,
Forget about anything,
For now we are one,
We have come together.

Emmanuella Okocha (10)
St Monica's RC Primary School, Hackney

Friendship

Friendship is a priceless gift
That cannot be bought or sold,
Its value is far greater than
A mountain made of gold.

For gold is very cold, it's lifeless,
It cannot speak nor hear
And when a time of triumph comes,
It will never, ever cheer.

So when you ask God for a gift,
Be thankful if he sends
Not diamonds, pearls or riches,
But the love of a real true friend.

Kemi Olawole (11)
St Monica's RC Primary School, Hackney

Is Somebody Out There Waiting For Me?

Is somebody out there waiting for me?
I am on my own, so don't scare me
I am very young for my age, I am only 10
I am very young and I live on my own
I only live with my teddy bear called Tracy
My parents passed away when I was young
My mum passed away when I was young
My dad's dead because he had a heart attack
I wish someone would adopt me and take me somewhere fun
I feel sorry for what happened
That's why I say
Is somebody out there waiting for me?

Rozel Frimpong
St Monica's RC Primary School, Hackney

Football

F ootball fans all out there
O ver the country everywhere
O ver the hills and everywhere
T o support their teams
B alls are used in different ways
A ll the teams are good
L ots of teams
L ots of fans overall.

Colee Hughes
St Monica's RC Primary School, Hackney

My Poems, All Poems

I feel my poems are special
    To me as well as you
Sometimes people may cry about them
    And maybe all life through

That's why it is said today
    That's also the happiest and best
For when it comes to poems
    My one outshines all the rest

Poems could be sad, happy or even rhythmless
    But mostly they make people cry
It doesn't matter if you want to be a writer or a poet
    As long as you always try!

Chanel Leadeham (11)
St Monica's RC Primary School, Hackney

Crawling Tortoise

Have you ever seen a tortoise crawling slowly,
Creeping slowly, fifty yards in half a day,
How so slowly, oh so slowly does he creep from place to place,
Tired look upon his face,
It is not because he is lazy
Or because he is old and slow,
If you were carrying a house,
How quickly would you go?

Veronica Philips (9)
St Monica's RC Primary School, Hackney

The Nightmare Six

Lurking in the darkness
Or in a dark cave
The nightmare six come out to being their deadly rave
Closet camper, chocolate chimp
Boogie bee, creepy crawler
Invisible cow and shy shrimp are their names
And one day hope they can be in the monster hall of fame
They will creep in your room
And turn off your night-light
Their methods are proven to scare you all night
But there is a way to stop this deadly crew
Take no showers for four days
And your stench will stop them from coming to you.

Kwadwo Amponsah
St Monica's RC Primary School, Hackney

I Love You

I would always stand by your side when you need help

L ove you like a mother loves its child
O ur love shall never end
V ery happy to be with you
E very day is a beautiful daydream

Y ou are my everything
O ne in a million lady
U nforgettable lady.

Obatare Uwegba
St Monica's RC Primary School, Hackney

Gone Too Soon

From the winter's wind
Wrecking the light
Here one day
Gone one night

By the floods
Of pouring rain
Here one day
Gone in pain

The autumn leaves
Yet to die
Here one day
Night rolls by.

Sheku Jalloh (11)
St Monica's RC Primary School, Hackney

Friendship

To give you a smile
Is me sharing my heart,
To give you a hug
Means I'll never be apart,
To stand by your side
Means that I care,
To give you my hand
Means I'll always be there.

Susan Le
St Monica's RC Primary School, Hackney

Why?

'Mummy, why are you a doctor?'
'Because it's my job'
'Why?'
'So we can have money'
'Why?'
'So we can move'
'Why?'
'So we can live somewhere else'
'Why?'
'So you live closer to your relatives'
'I'm tired of saying 'Why?''
'Why?'

Temi Soyinka (11)
St Monica's RC Primary School, Hackney

Friendship

You are my friend, I will never forget you
If you leave me please do not forget me
If you have already, it will really hurt me
Sometimes I think you will never come back.

Alexia Oladipo
St Monica's RC Primary School, Hackney

Poems

P eaches are orange.
O ranges look like porridge.
E at them and you will feel better.
M y friend is writing a letter.
S o that's how it ends, see you again.

Alistair Mark
St Monica's RC Primary School, Hackney

Jacqueline Wilson

Jacqueline Wilson is my favourite author
When I read her books I'm in the sky
Jacqueline Wilson is my favourite author
And this is the reason why

She has a sense of fantasy
And a special sense of humour
Her books are so interesting
It would be an offence to put it down

Oh, I'm so dangerous in love with her books
I can hardly contain myself
That's when I see her books in the library
I nearly take the whole shelf

My favourite book is Double Act
Which is about two twins who can never be separated
But one day when they both get accepted at two
                    different secondary schools
That's when the battle begins

I've read 15 of her books
As you can see I'm her greatest fan
Jacqueline Wilson has inspired me in many, many ways
That's why she's my favourite author

I know Jacqueline's inside and out
And even when she was born
I even know all her hobbies
Even the name of her mummy!

I know when her first book was published
I know her mission is accomplished
So there you go, that's one of the lessons she's taught me
If you put your mind to anything, you can achieve it.

Grace Adeyemi (11)
St Monica's RC Primary School, Hackney

Some Children Are . . .

Door-slammers
Plate-smashers
Window-crackers
Vegetable-haters
Day-dreamers
Football-kickers
Jump-ropers
Chatter-boxes
Street-crowders
Tree-climbers
Trouble-makers
Story-lovers
Pencil-sharpeners
Cry-babies
TV-hoggers
Havoc-wreckers
Tell-tales
Cake-chompers
Candy-eaters
Pet-cuddlers

(But all of us have something in common,
A wild imagination!)

Uchenna Ekemezie
St Monica's RC Primary School, Hackney

Little Kitty

Little kitty
What a pity
Playing with a bone
Why don't you eat some fish
And leave my leg alone?

Jordan Abraham (10)
St Monica's RC Primary School, Hackney

Life

Life is a noise, it's beautifully free
So natural like the Earth's tiny killer bee
I'll understand one day but for now
I pray every day may we be able to play
Life is not easy, is it hard?
Tremendously, one way or the other
We get through it
Maybe it's long and hard
But bit by bit, sooner or later
We will all be gone
Stop putting people through misery
You'll perish one by one.

Rocksea Ogefere
St Monica's RC Primary School, Hackney

When

'When are we going to KFC?
When are we going to Dave's?
When are we going to get my birthday present?
When are we going shopping?
When are we going? Mum, are you listening?'
'Uh!'

Oreadura Soyinka (9)
St Monica's RC Primary School, Hackney

The Toyshop

Once upon a very long time,
When the clock at midnight gave a booming chime,
Toys in the nursery all came to life,
Big fluffy teddy and his small fat wife.

Up popped bouncy Jack-in-the-box,
With all his tumbling curly locks,
This did not please the kangaroo,
So he jumped up and shouted 'Boo!'

Twirling and swishing came the slim dancing doll,
Known to the others as Graceful Moll,
Round in a circle went the clockwork train,
Past a tin station without any name.

Twenty-two soldiers march to the right,
All in a straight line ready to fight
And last but not least came sad old clown,
In his circus costume of yellow and brown.

The toys had fun the whole night long,
Finishing up by singing a song,
They played for hours in sheer delight,
Till in through the window streamed morning light.

Then cuckoo clock warned it was time to stop,
The owner soon would return to the shop,
'Back to your places,' screamed Barbie doll Jill
And all the toys were once again still.

Niriksha Bharadia (10)
Summerside Primary School, North Finchley

A Tale Of A Tail

This is a tale
About a tail,
A tail belonging to a squirrel,
A squirrel called Mr Wirrel.

Now he was a fairy
And people found him scary,
But not these two, Nick and Sam,
They acted as though he was a lamb.

He gave them wishes,
(Once even fishes),
But last night said Nick,
'I wish there were Vikings,
So come on, quick.'

Yes, came the Vikings
(And not to Sam's liking),
They had to fight,
Until came night.

There were still six more,
But less than before.
Said Sam, 'I don't like the squirrel,
The horrid, mean Wirrel!'

So when the Vikings all had been fought,
The children both went and the squirrel they caught.
They hung him on a length of wire
And his tail came off which was his desire!

His tail is here to this very day,
But Mr Wirrel, he's run away!

Charmian Chong (10)
Summerside Primary School, North Finchley

Get A Life!

Sly lies and snide asides
Knife-edged whispers to slice through my confidence
Sneaky tricks to try and make me feel small
Malicious mutterings, poisoning minds
Silent sniggers among your chosen ones
Watching me
Watching me
The slightest mistake, a silly slip
You're there and laughing
All the time
If you despise me
It's a surprise to me
That you waste your time on me
If you're so cool
Aren't you being a fool
To bother with me?

Why don't you just get a life
And leave me alone!

Elisa De Luca (10)
Summerside Primary School, North Finchley

A Lion

I hate being in a cage
With people staring at me all the time
The same meat and vegetables for dinner
I hate it
I don't get any freedom
Or any privacy
I hate it
I wonder why they do this to us lions?
I wonder how they would like it if I did the same to them?
I wonder . . . ?

Alice Parsons (9)
Vita Et Pax School, Southgate

Seven Little Children

Seven little children
Building with bricks
One got hit on the head
And then there were six

Six little children
Ready to dive
One went away
And then there were five

Five little children
Went on tour
One got stung
And then there were four

Four little children
Climb a tree
One got stuck
And then there were three

Three little children
Going to the loo
One fell in
And then there were two

Two little children
Playing in the sun
One got stolen
And then there was one

One little child
Swimming for fun
She got lost
And hen there were none.

George O'Shea (7)
Vita Et Pax School, Southgate

Seven Little Children

Seven little children
Building houses with bricks
One went home
And then there were six

Six little children
Try and get a hive
One got insured
And then there were five

Five little children
Going to the shore
One got lost
And then there were four

Four little children
Went to get a bee
One got stung
And then there were three

Three little children
Cleaning their shoe
One went home
And then there were two

Two little children
Having fun
One fainted
And then there was one.

May Araki (7)
Vita Et Pax School, Southgate

Seven Little Children

Seven little children
Went to play with some Lego bricks
One had to go home
And then there were six

Six little children
Went to play with a beehive
One ran away
And then there were five

Five little children
Went to the video store
One got lost
And then there were four

Four little children
Climbed a tree
One fell down
And then there were three

Three little children
Went to the loo
One got lost
And then there were two

Two little children
Holding a ton
One got squashed
And then there was one

One little child
Eating a bun
He got too fat
And then there were none.

Joseph Kruczkowski (8)
Vita Et Pax School, Southgate

Seven Little Children

Seven little children
Going to get pick 'n' mix
One fell down the toilet
And then there were six

Six little children
Looking for a beehive
One got lost
And then there were five

Five little children
Going on a tour
One got knocked down
And then there were four

Four little children
Chasing a bee
One got stung
And then there were three

Three little children
Standing in a queue
One went home
And then there were two

Two little children
Playing with a toy gun
One got bored
And then there was one

One little child
Tanning in the sun
Then went swimming
And then there were none!

Theana Gregoriou (7)
Vita Et Pax School, Southgate

Seven Little Children

Seven little children
Going to fix some bricks
One went to the toilet
And then there were six

Six little children
Looking at a beehive
One got stung
And then there were five

Five little children
Knocking on a door
One ran away
And then there were four

Four little children
Sitting in a tree
One fell off
And then there were three

Three little children
Going to the loo
One stayed in there
And then there were two

Two little children
Chewing some gum
One spat his out
And then there was one

One little child
Watching Finding Nemo
He fell asleep
And then there were none.

Aasar Patel (7)
Vita Et Pax School, Southgate

Seven Little Children

Seven little children
Standing on some bricks
One fell over
And then there were six

Six little children
Playing in a hive
One got stung
And then there were five

Five little children
Going on a tour
One fainted
And then there were four

Four little children
Catching fleas
One got bit
And then there were three

Three little children
Going to the loo
One got flushed
And then there were two

Two little children
Eating a bun
One got poisoned
And then there was one

One little child
Going for a run
Then he felt sick
And there were none.

Kishen Patel (7)
Vita Et Pax School, Southgate

Seven Little Children

Seven little children
Going to buy pick 'n' mix
One fell over
And then there were six

Six little children
That were all alive
One got a heart attack
And then there were five

Five little children
On a tour
One got knocked out
And then there were four

Four little children
Going for a wee
One got flushed
And then there were three

Three little children
Drinking hot stew
One got burnt
And then there were two

Two little children
Having lots of fun
One walked away
And then there was one

One little child
Bathing in the sun
He went swimming
And then there were none.

Zaid Hussain (8)
Vita Et Pax School, Southgate

Seven Little Children

Seven little children
Sitting on some bricks
One fell off
And then there were six

Six little children
Poking at a hive
One got stung
And then there were five

Five little children
Opened a door
One hit his head
And then there were four

Four little children
Sitting in a tree
One fell out
And then there were three

Three little children
Sitting on the loo
One got flushed down
And then there were two

Two little children
Eating a bun
One was poisoned
And then there was one

One little child
Having fun
He got stuck
And then there were none.

Isabella Chan (8)
Vita Et Pax School, Southgate

St Patrick's Day

Seventeenth March is St Patrick's Day
In Ireland - he is our patron Saint
Shamrock proudly worn on coats
The Irish in London at work they ain't

There's Irish dance and diddley music
In pubs all over town
And you'll never find on Paddy's Day
A sober man around

Guinness hats are standing tall
Football jerseys very green
Laughing, joking, cheering crowds
Meeting friends not lately seen

St Patrick's Day reminds us all
Of family and friends across the sea
They have a ball - they do not work
On St Paddy's Day they're full of glee.

Brogan McAuliffe (8)
Vita Et Pax School, Southgate

Ant

I am a very lucky creature, I have freedom.
When all my friends come round, it attracts children.
If only we could have a rest, I work *so* hard.
The best thing about me is that I am free but I get treated badly.

Connor Ellerbeck (8)
Vita Et Pax School, Southgate

The Athlete

The nerves at the beginning start to set in;
She loosens up her muscles and kisses her cross,
Wishes her opponents good look,
Focuses on the finishing line.
Kisses her cross one more time,
Bang! The gun goes, she sprints,
Muscles suddenly feel beefy,
Her leg muscles rippling with anticipation to win this race.
She's got 30 metres left,
She's in the lead, closely followed by her main competitor.
She suddenly sprints and tears away from her competitor,
She's delighted, nearly there.
She's won!
The crowd roars!
She then collapses on the floor,
Picks herself up slowly,
Kisses her cross for the last time,
Goes to collect her medal and the crowd roars,
That was a strong mighty run, she thinks to herself.

Nneka Ezekude (9)
Vita Et Pax School, Southgate

The Athlete

His eyes are focused as can be,
Jumping all around the place.
His muscles bouncing around,
The crowd are excited,
Kissing his good luck charms.
Bang! He starts slowly but in first place,
His running was hasty and suddenly dashed to the finish line,
The crowd roared,
The runner walked for a lap of honour,
Then he collected his trophy and lifted it up over his head,
Then proudly strolled to the dressing room.

Ben Calder (8)
Vita Et Pax School, Southgate

The Athlete

The runner was expanding his muscles, loosening them,
He was focusing on the finishing line,
His heart was heavily pounding,
He was tanned from the sun,
Rippling muscles with a six pack and beefy,
The runner gets in his start position,
He's terrified,
The starter raised his gun, *bang!*
The runner sprang off, he was surging towards the finish line,
He alofted his arms in enjoyment and delight,
The crowd roared for the athlete and clapped their hands,
The runner got awarded a cup
And walked proudly to the dressing room.

Max Hannington (9)
Vita Et Pax School, Southgate

Teacher's Prayers

Let the children be in our hands
And make them listen to our commands,
Come to school on time each day
And don't make me say, 'You're late today!'
Don't let them talk in the hall,
Or talk in front of the headmaster, Mr Paul,
Tell them not to drop crumbs on the floor
And don't let them come in without knocking on the door,
Please may you make them respect me,
As you can see, Lord, this is my prayer.

Asagi Nakata (8)
Vita Et Pax School, Southgate

The Athlete

Stretching his muscles before the race,
His heart pouncing heavily,
Focusing on the finish line,
Victory in his eyes.
The starter raises his gun slowly,
The crowd falls silent
Bang!
He leapt forward,
The crowd was ecstatic,
He charged round the track,
Bolting past everyone,
He was as swift as an arrow,
He was winning!
The finish line was 100m away,
He ran with all his might,
He dashed past the finish line,
He had come first!
The judge awarded him with a gold trophy,
He raised it in victory,
He scampered intro the changing room,
He had *won!*

Savva Spanos (9)
Vita Et Pax School, Southgate

Thierry Henry

On the field his legs are magic
He scores when least expected
Henry is the slickest player
The coaches speak glowing terms
They all want to sign my hero, Henry.

Jason McKenna (9)
Vita Et Pax School, Southgate

All Animals!

Elephant grey and big
Not as greedy as a pig
Tiger with its fierce roar
It will never, ever hurt its paw
Pig, greedy and shy
One day you might even see it cry
Giraffe, tall as it can be
I wonder if it can touch a tree?
Rabbit, smooth and soft
You might even find one in your loft
Rhinoceros, fierce and strong
We always say that they are wrong
Camel, long and bumpy
I should think they're quite grumpy
Cheetah, spotty and fast
Never like it when they're last
Bear, strong and fat
Should be quite the opposite of a rat
Spider, hairy and small
You just can't hear them when they call!

Artsitha Kailayapathivagan (8)
Vita Et Pax School, Southgate

River Poem

The river meanders down the hill,
Slowly twisting like a snake,
Crashing across the big black rocks,
Sailors are screaming for help,
Suddenly it stops
And the river becomes calm,
Children playing in the water,
Singing river songs,
Beautiful fish jumping up and down,
Just like a calm river.

Karidia Papapetrou (11)
Vita Et Pax School, Southgate

Evacuation

She stands on the smoking platform for the last time,
The station is like a zoo crowded with animals,
Feeling sad, lost and not knowing what to do.
Her mother worried about her children, holding back her tears,
Wishes she could chase after her children
And bring them back.
Her little brother not knowing why everyone's so upset,
He thinks this is like a holiday,
But he wonders where his mother is.
The train steaming up, nearly ready to move,
Clouds of smoke puff up, then the whistle shrieks,
Feeling sad and scared, saying her last goodbyes.
Staring through the window at the green trees of Wales,
She thinks of her mother and father,
She remembers her family,
She wonders if her family will be reunited,
She hopes this is all a dream and she will wake
And find her family with no war.
The destination was long but about to end,
She waits silently until she is picked,
Not to leave her brother,
Children chosen, she is the last one,
Only with her brother.

Christina Theoharous (10)
Vita Et Pax School, Southgate

Black

Black is a dark colour
It means dullness
It is the colour of lots of things
Like chocolate
Raisins and sunglasses
Black is not a bright colour
Or a light colour
But it is still my favourite colour.

Joe Lanario (10)
Vita Et Pax School, Southgate

Snow

Snow falls on top of trees
The bitter cold shakes your knees
Houses look like birthday cakes
With loads and loads of snowflakes

Snow piles on top of your car
So you can't get very far
It forms a blanket over grass
It turns to ice like a pane of glass

Hard ponds and frozen lakes
This is what Jack Frost makes
Children for school can be late
While their parents just skate

Little children wear mitts
While big vehicles drop grit
Animals hibernate in cold weather
While snow is as soft as a feather

People play in snow
But you must know
That you cannot run
Or it won't be fun

And last of all it is Yuletide
When people snuggle up inside
I really love the *snow*
It fills me with a glow!

David Alam   (9)
Vita Et Pax School, Southgate

Evacuation

She stands on the platform
The station is like a flock of people
Feeling sad and heartbroken
Her mother breathless and shocked that her
Children are going away
Her little brother not knowing what's going on
The train whistling away puffing smoke out
Feeling upset and anxious

Staring through the cloudy windows
Seeing huge hills and brightly coloured flowers
She thinks of her mum, the look on her face
Tears falling down
She remembers all the good times she had with her brothers
She wonders which family she'll go with
She hopes her family will be safe in London from all the bombing

Destination: the train stops
As the children leave the train and into a hall
She waits still, her heart beating
As chunks of children stand in the hall happily.

Amy Cooke (9)
Vita Et Pax School, Southgate

Walking On

I walk down the cold, wooden stairs,
Dusty-blue curtains tied in pairs,
I tread on the hard marbles left from yesterday,
On the soft, silky socks which are pipe smoke-grey,
My hand scrapes the wall, crusty but still and dry,
I tread on a stick, it starts to cry,
I splash in a puddle, the tears fly out,
Crack goes a seed, I stepped on it, would it sprout?
Into a park which stands for me,
Little, fat robin I can see,
Should I walk on until I fall off this earth?

Makoto Nakata (9)
Vita Et Pax School, Southgate

Evacuation

She stands on the dusty platform,
The station's full of confused children.
Acting very brave, but anxious and upset,
Her mother struggles to keep her tears back,
Giving her children a warm hug, lets them go.

Her little brother's full of excitement,
Not knowing what's going on,
The train generating clouds and clouds of steam,
Moves away into the distance,
Feeling distressed and upset, she is full of sorrow,
Peering through the steamed-up window,
At continuous lush green fields,
With cows munching away at the grass,
She thinks of her friends back in the village,
Not forgetting her mother's feelings.

She remembers the good times with her family,
Gathered around the warm log fire, listening to the radio,
She thinks about her father,
Engaged in the blood-splattered battle across from English shores,
She anticipates and waits for the family reunion,
Destination Wales; the train chugs into the peaceful station,
She waits, apprehensively not knowing where she and her brother will
End up.

One by one, two by two the children go,
Her main concern is her brother,
Trembling with fear not knowing what to do,
She steps off the train squeezing her brother's hand
As securely as she can.

Vikesh Anil Patel (10)
Vita Et Pax School, Southgate

Mr McGee

Old Mr McGee climbed up a tree,
Then fell down and broke his knee,
Once he climbed up a chimney which was very tall
And then was hit down by the school football.
He once saved Mrs Green's cat called Nic-Nak,
By prodding himself with a very sharp tack,
That 'old timer' is a saint you can see,
Good ol' Mr McGee

Old Mr McGee is now eighty-three
He really is a sight to see
He knows things that nobody knows
Alas he also has his woes
That 'old timer' is a saint you can see
Good ol' Mr McGee

Old Mr McGee has departed us
Now I have to catch the bus
My homework is in piles now
Because Mr McGee is not around to show us how
Mr McGee is now dead
And we will always remember the day we said
'Good ol' Mr McGee'

It is hard to believe yesterday we leapt
And all we have done today is wept
That 'old timer' was a saint you could see
Good ol' Mr McGee.

Nicholas Wilson (9)
Vita Et Pax School, Southgate

The Enchanted Tree

Inside my garden
There's an enchanted tree
Where little elves sit next to me

I knock on the door and wait
For the king of the fairies
He's my best mate

Inside of the tree
Me and the king dance with glee
We await the coming of the princess
She's got a magic dress

Soon I have to go
I leave the enchanted tree
Of pure
Magic!

Monique Clarke (10)
Vita Et Pax School, Southgate

Coca-Cola

Hail O Coca-Cola
Most wonderful of all
Your elegant figure
Is so divine
And your fizzy bubbles
Pop in my mouth
With your vanilla and cherry flavours
Make me go hyper
My mouth would be dry
Without your marvellous flavour
Never shall I drink another lemonade
Never shall I gulp another orange juice
Never shall I touch another drink
You are the king of all drinks.

Brooke Elder (11)
Vita Et Pax School, Southgate

Evacuation

She stands on the platform,
The station is packed with hundreds of children being evacuated.
Feeling very small, she tries to stop the sobbing inside her.
Her mother, holding back her tears, gripping her children tightly,
She wishes she could change time.
Her little brother saying goodbye to his mother excitedly,
Not knowing what is happening.
The train is leaving the station, taking children to safety.
Feeling sad inside, she looks like she does not care,
She does not say goodbye, just sits there, thinking about the future.
Staring dreamily through the steamy window, she sees bushes
But in the background she is filled with sorrow
While watching two people waving, while tending their flock,
Standing in front of the large Welsh hills.
She thinks of her mum and her little brother running and playing
In the leafy fields.
She wishes she was at home warming up to the small fire,
Sitting next to her mother.
She remembers the times before the war,
She wishes those times would return.
Destination, she wonders where she is, the train stops suddenly,
She waits, wishing she would be taken home,
While watching children leaving to new homes,
Soon the hall is empty, she is one of the last children left.

Antonia Lambis (9)
Vita Et Pax School, Southgate

Ode To A Motor Car

Hail to the motor car most speedy of them all
Your sleek metal caging so divine
Aston Martin what a beast, Ferrari what a demon
Ford GT what a blast, never will be beaten
TVR roaring through, Mercedes what a star
Oh, I wish I had a car!

Leo Chadwell (11)
Vita Et Pax School, Southgate

The River

The river is fast,
The river has a task.

The river is sparkling in the sun,
The river is bubbling.

The river is gurgling,
The river is twisting and turning,
Beating the canoe.

The river calms down and flows,
Through the brown woods.

The river is flowing with a gentle push,
The river needs to do a gentle deed,
The children play with happiness and joy in its stream.

Kirtiman Singh (11)
Vita Et Pax School, Southgate

Ode To A Malteser

Hail to a Malteser,
I honour you with praise.
Your smooth coating
Over your crunchy inside.
Your circular shape
Fits my mouth perfectly.
Your crunch makes my eyes fill with joy,
Your flavour is so divine,
You are the royal relish.

Esther Cameron (11)
Vita Et Pax School, Southgate

A River I Know

The river is a dancer,
Watch it slowly curl,
But be careful not to anger it
Or get on its nerves,
Many tributaries it owns,
Watch the way the river flows,
Suddenly the river bubbles,
We've hit turbulence,
The river bends round,
Left . . . right . . . left . . . right,
Endlessly,
The river thunders down the waterfall
And down the narrow valley,
It roars like a lion,
Spits like a cobra,
All the way to the mouth,
It finally reaches the sea,
Advancing and retreating
From the shore.

Craigg Thompson (11)
Vita Et Pax School, Southgate

The River

The river is a fish,
Looping and twisting to the roaring sea.
It sparkles, meandering through,
On a dark starry night,
With quiet night sky sounds,
Bending round the rocky corner,
Rolling towards the steep fall, crashing down.
Salmon hopping, twisting, like the wind in the sky,
Reaching its destination, the monstrous sea.

Andrew Nicholas (11)
Vita Et Pax School, Southgate

A River's Journey

Way, way up in the dark, imposing mountains
A little spring bubbles and trickles and gently slides
                        down the mountainside
But this weak trickle of water will soon become
A cascading torrent of destructive power
In the form of a huge snake-like river
Winding its way across the lush western European countryside

As this little trickle of water is spilling down the mountains
More and more little isolated streams attach themselves
To this small body of water adding to the momentum and
                        force of this little river
The river starts to dislodge small pebbles and stones of ever
                        increasing weight and mass
Due to the increasing amount of tributaries contributing to
                        this river's momentum, force and volume
Once a small inquisitive lamb gently touched the dark, sinister surface
Of the water and a small sharp stone surfaced at a speed
Only matched by a jet effectively signing its death warrant

As the final stages of the river's journey approach
The countryside shook with fear as the dark, domineering figure
Of the winding river crashes against the rocks
And finally hits the seemingly endless sea
With the force of a thousand fully-sized elephants stomping
                        on the earth
This is the story of just one river as I see it in my head
However there are many in the world and they are not all like this.

Harrison Hutchinson (11)
Vita Et Pax School, Southgate

The River

The river is flowing slowly, drifting past silently,
Gurgling with pride, lashes round corners as the sun blares down,
Looping on the hills and bubbles as it goes down,
Twists and turns, sparkling with a flash,
Then it slows down on the rocks,
Trickling off the stones, a fish swims past with frogs jumping,
Then it gradually gets faster, swerving round and round.

We're nearly there, then splash, it flows into the sea,
Calmly it foams, drifting off,
Giant whales jumping up and down meeting it silently,
The water meets the fish and gurgles with pride,
Then the stars come out, meeting the darkness,
Sparkling down to the river.

Alexandra Tranmer (10)
Vita Et Pax School, Southgate

The River

The river meanders down the hill
Slowly curving and slightly twisting
Gurgling like a happy baby
Frogs and newts bathe in its waters

The river splashes and crashes
As it hits the limestone rocks
Boats are flying everywhere
Sailors are crying for help

Suddenly the storm comes to a halt
As the river plunges into the *big, deep* sea
On its way it has passed villages and cities
And at last it is here!

Natasha Patel (10)
Vita Et Pax School, Southgate

The Meanings Of Colours

Red is the colour of evil
That is watching us from Hell

Yellow is the colour of the sun
Shining down above us

Pink is the colour of happiness
Which fills our hearts joyfully

Green is the colour of the outdoors
Mile upon mile of land

Black is the colour of sadness
It reminds us of nothing

Purple is the colour of holiness
It is a peaceful colour

Blue is the colour of the sky
Without the clouds in its way.

Hannah Brown (10)
Vita Et Pax School, Southgate

Ode To A Malteser

Hail chocolate Malteser,
Most delicious of them all,
Your circular figure,
As round as a ball,
Your chocolate coating
And crunchy inside,
Makes my taste buds go wild and mad,
I love the Malteser,
Your texture,
Your taste,
Fill my mouth with delight,
Hail O Malteser,
You're the best of them all . . .

Sara Bolognini (11)
Vita Et Pax School, Southgate

Boring, Boring, Boring

There's nothing left for me to do,
I'm bored of them,
I'm bored of you.

I'm bored of being in my room,
I'm bored of sitting in the gloom.

I'm bored of bed,
I'm bored of food,
I'm bored of being in a mood.

I'm bored of sky,
I'm bored of rain,
I'm bored of everything the same.

I'm bored of milk,
I'm bored of bread,
I feel as if I'm boring dead.

I'm bored of poems,
I'm bored of rhymes,
About all my boring times.

I'm bored of my computer too,
Cos there's nothing left for me to do.

Stephanie Lykourgou (10)
Vita Et Pax School, Southgate

Ode To Haribo

Hail O Haribo
We bow to you
You're so chewy and wonderful
The different coloured sweets
A variety of tastes
Fill my mouth
Never shall I touch another toffee
Or another chewy sweet
For you are the king of sweets.

Cameron Willcock (11)
Vita Et Pax School, Southgate

The Athlete

Her sweaty hands firmly gripping her new red hockey stick,
Beads of sweat trickling down her thoughtful, determined face.
Her lucky trainers tied up in small, neat bows,
It all depends on the one penalty goal she is taking,
Will she score or will she have an unlucky miss?
Who knows?

Walking slowly to the penalty line,
Focusing her eyes on the small ball,
Ears pricked up listening for the sharp, piercing sound of the whistle,
Screech!
There it goes,
The crowd hold their breath,
Waiting in silence,
Positioning her stick,
She slices it through the air,
Bringing it purposely down to the ground,
She aims,
Hitting the ball forcefully with her stick,
She steps back and watches the ball skimming the pitch.

The ball glides through the air
And into the opposing team's net!
'She scores' called the ecstatic commentator,
Smiling and waving to the cheering crowd surrounding her,
She walks into the dressing room,
Knowing that she had won her team the match.

Stella Spanos (10)
Vita Et Pax School, Southgate

Seven Little Children

Seven little children
Trying to do some tricks
One vanished another
And then there were six

Six little children
Walking near a hive
One got stung
And then there were five

Five little children
Fighting in a war
One got killed
And then there were four

Four little children
Looking out to sea
One gets eaten by a shark
And then there were three

Three little children
Going to the loo
One got flushed down
And then there were two

Two little children
Having fun in the sun
One drowned in the water
And then there was one

One little child
Not having fun
He went back home
And then there were none.

Amaarah Hossain (7)
Vita Et Pax School, Southgate

My Favourite Things

Cars that are zooming
PlayStation games booming
Cartoons on telly
My socks that are smelly
These are a few of my favourite things

Chocolate and sweets
All sorts of treats
Wobbly jelly
Filling my belly
These are a few of my favourite things

Rugby and football
Going to school
Playing with friends
Making secret dens
These are a few of my favourite things.

Max Brown (7)
Vita Et Pax School, Southgate

Ode To Popcorn

Hail O sweet popcorn,
The highest of all flavours,
Divine your fresh white colour,
So clean and super, your taste can vary,
Toffee, salt, sweet,
It is too hard to choose,
Your delicious flavour makes my taste buds
Fill up with joy to their limits,
If you ever were to leave me, my sweet one,
I wouldn't know what to do,
Without you, watching the scary movies wouldn't be the same,
I shall never touch a toffee,
I shall never touch a chew,
I shall never touch a mint,
For you will always stay number one, top of the *pop!*

Tara McSharry (11)
Vita Et Pax School, Southgate

Seven Little Children

Seven little children
Going for a pick 'n' mix
One ate a Twix
And then there were six

Six little children
Going to a hive
One got stung
And then there were five

Five little children
Going on a tour
One fell off
And then there were four

Four little children
Playing with a bee
One got stung
And then there were three

Three little children
Going to the loo
One got flushed down
And then there were two

Two little children
Going for a run
One fell over
And then there was one

One little child
Eating a bun
He threw up
And then there were none.

Euan O'Sullivan-Biggar (8)
Vita Et Pax School, Southgate

Seven Little Children

Seven little children
Building with bricks
One was too lazy
And then there were six

Six little children
Playing alive
One dived into a dustbin
And then there were five

Five little children
Knocking on the door
One saw a candy man
And then there were four

Four little children
Doing a wee
One got stolen
And then there were three

Three little children
Playing with goo
One fell into a swimming pool
And then there were two

Two little children
Showing their bums
One got stung
And then there was one

One little child
Sitting in the sun
He got burnt
And then there were none.

Jack Anthonisz (8)
Vita Et Pax School, Southgate

Seven Little Children

Seven little children
Picking up sticks
One got lost
And then there were six

Six little children
Jumping on a hive
One had an accident
And then there were five

Five little children
One was poor
They were homeless
And then there were four

Four little children
Playing near a tree
One got hurt
And then there were three

Three little children
Drinking hot stew
One got burnt
And then there were two

Two little children
Having lots of fun
One walked away
And then there was one

One little child
Not having fun
He'd lost his friends
And then there were none!

Ziana Mitha (7)
Vita Et Pax School, Southgate